"I am tempted to say that this is no ordinary book. In a culture that rhapsodizes over every achievement and idolizes many of those who stand out, it is easy for the church to drink from the same intoxicating elixir and swoon over gifted exceptions. How refreshing to read a book that tries to locate spiritual and theological maturity in ordinary faith and obedience, in ordinary relationships, in ordinary service, in ordinary pastors. Michael Horton does not mean to depreciate believers with exceptional gifts, but he rightly warns us against erecting shrines to them — shrines that blind us to the glory of the gospel worked out in the faithful discipleship of 'ordinary' Christian living, shrines that make us forget we serve a God who will not give his glory to another. That we need a book like this is more than a little sad; the book that addresses the problem wisely and well is, frankly, extraordinary."

— **D. A. Carson, Research Professor of New Testament, Trinity Evangelical Divinity School**

"Michael Horton's *Ordinary* is, well, extraordinary. It can be described in many ways, and one is this: a call to love God and neighbor in freedom and grace, in the neighborhood you already inhabit, with the gifts and talents (and weaknesses!) you already possess. Spiritual heroes need not apply."

— **Mark Galli, Editor, *Christianity Today***

"In an age of 'radicals' always promising us the next best thing, Michael Horton wisely and winsomely points us to God's faithfulness in the ordinary means of grace. In an era where everyone seems to have a nonprofit start-up that aims to ⬚⬚⬚⬚⬚⬚⬚ ⬚ ⬚⬚⬚ ton reminds us of the joy found in ord⬚ gations where the Spirit dwells. In an be writing their memoir, Horton show that quietly but faithfully care for los⬚ thing'; God is at work in small, good things."

— **James K. A. Smith, Gary & Henrietta Byker Chair in Applied Reformed Theology & Worldview, Calvin College**

Her finely-touched spirit had still its fine issues, though they were not widely visible. Her full nature, like that of which Cyrus broke the strength, spent itself in channels which had no great name on the earth. But the effect of her being on those around her was incalculably diffusive: for the growing good of the world is partly dependent on unhistoric acts; and that things are not so ill with you and me as they might have been, is half owing to the number who lived faithfully a hidden life, and rest in unvisited tombs.

—Conclusion to George Eliot's *Middlemarch*

or·di·nar·y

Sustainable Faith in a Radical,
Restless World

MICHAEL HORTON

ZONDERVAN

Ordinary
Copyright © 2014 by Michael S. Horton

This title is also available as a Zondervan ebook.
Visit www.zondervan.com/ebooks.

This title is also available in a Zondervan audio edition.
Visit www.zondervan.fm.

Requests for information should be addressed to:

Zondervan, 3900 *Sparks Dr. SE, Grand Rapids, Michigan 49546*

Library of Congress Cataloging-in-Publication Data

Horton, Michael Scott.
    Ordinary : sustaining faith in a radical, restless world / Michael Horton.
        pages cm
    ISBN 978-0-310-51737-5
    1. Christian life. I. Title.
BV4501.3.H6774 2014
    248.4 — dc23   2014010371

Cover design: FaceOut Studio
Interior design: David Conn

Printed in the United States of America

14 15 16 17 18 19 20 21 22 23 24 /DCI/ 20 19 18 17 16 15 14 13 12 11 10 9 8 7 6 5 4

contents

acknowledgments

I owe special thanks for the final form of this book to my editors at Zondervan, Ryan Pazdur and Verlyn Verbrugge. Along the way, the manuscript was improved by the wit and wisdom of a great friend, Judith Riddell, although remaining weaknesses should not be imputed to her. As always, I am grateful to the Lord for my wife and children, who make the ordinary special, and to pastors Michael Brown and Zachary Keele for their dedication to the ordinary means of grace.

PART 1

radical and restless

CHAPTER 1

the new radical

Radical. Epic. Revolutionary.
Transformative. Impactful. Life-Changing.
Ultimate. Extreme. Awesome.
Emergent. Alternative. Innovative.
On The Edge. The Next Big Thing. Explosive Breakthrough.

You can probably add to the list of modifiers that have become, ironically, part of the *ordinary* conversations in society and in today's church. Most of us have heard expressions like these so often that they've become background noise. We tune them out, unconsciously doubting what is offered because it has become so predictably common. As my grammar teacher used to say, "If you make every sentence an exclamation or put every verb in 'bold,' then nothing stands out."

To grab—and hold—our attention, everything has to have an exclamation point. We've become accustomed to looking around restlessly for something new, the latest and greatest, that idea or product or person or experience that will solve our problems, give us some purpose, and change the world. Although we might be a little jaded by the ads, we're eager to take whatever it is "to a whole new level."

"Ordinary" has to be one of the loneliest words in our vocabulary today. Who wants a bumper sticker that announces to the neighborhood, "My child is an ordinary student at Bubbling Brook Elementary"? Who wants to be that ordinary person who lives in an ordinary town, is a member of an ordinary church, and has ordinary friends and works an ordinary job? Our life has to *count*! We have to leave our mark, have a legacy, and make a difference. And all of this should be something that can be managed, measured, and maintained. We have to live up to our Facebook profile. It's one of the newer versions of salvation by works.

Still, I sense a growing restlessness with this restlessness. Some have grown tired of the constant calls to radical change through new and improved schemes. They are less sure they want to jump on the next bandwagon or trail-blaze new paths to greatness. You know that something's afoot when a satirical newspaper like *The Onion* pokes fun at this fad, reducing our hyperbolic lives to a sarcastic joke:

CAMDEN, ME—Longtime acquaintances confirmed to reporters this week that local man Michael Husmer, an unambitious 29-year-old loser who leads an enjoyable and fulfilling life, still lives in his hometown and has no desire to leave.

Claiming that the aimless slouch has never resided more than two hours from his parents and still hangs out with friends from high school, sources close to Husmer reported that the man, who has meaningful, lasting personal relationships and a healthy work-life balance, is an unmotivated washout who's perfectly comfortable being a nobody for the rest of his life.

"I've known Mike my whole life and he's a good guy, but it's pretty pathetic that he's still living on the same street he grew up on and experiencing a deep sense of personal satisfaction," childhood friend David Gorman said of the unaspiring, completely gratified do-nothing. "As soon as Mike graduated from college, he moved back home and started working at a local insurance firm. Now, he's nearly 30 years old, living in the exact same town he was born in, working at the same small-time job, and is extremely contented in all aspects of his home and professional lives. It's really sad." ... Additionally, pointing to the intimate, enduring connections he's developed with his wife, parents, siblings, and neighbors, sources reported that Husmer's life is "pretty humiliating" on multiple levels.

Husmer's ordinary life is debt-free and he is perfectly content to stay put while many of his high school friends go off to the bright lights and big cities. He doesn't care about impressing total strangers every day as he climbs the corporate ladder, when he can invest in the lives of those closest to him. He doesn't have a thousand "friends" on Facebook, just a close family and circle of friends in town. "I'm just glad I got out of there and didn't end up like Mike," said Husmer's cousin Amary Martin, 33, an attorney at a large law firm who hasn't seen Husmer, her closest childhood playmate, for nearly six years. "The last thing I'd ever want is to have a loving family nearby, feel a sense of pleasure when reflecting on my life, and be the big failure that everyone runs into when they visit home once a year for the holidays."[1]

There is a lot of truth in the portrait of "poor" Mike Husmer. Ironically, today, it isn't all that difficult to pull up roots, and become anonymous — starting life all over — with a new set of relationships. Our mobile, individualistic culture makes it possible for us to reinvent ourselves whenever we want a fresh start and a new set of supporting actors in our personalized life movie.

Even the Lego company piled on with a blockbuster 2014 film that parodies the culture of corporate hype of which it is a part. As one review of *The Lego Movie* explains, "It's about a Lego minifigure named Emmet, whose empty mind has been filled with a blind devotion to an indifferent commercial empire. Thanks to the evil mastermind known as President Business (and later, Lord Business), Emmet watches the same stupid TV shows and listens to the same insipid pop songs over and over again ('Everything is awesome!'. . .)."[2] At the end of the movie/infomercial, Emmet appeals to Lord Business: "You don't have to be the bad guy. You are the most talented, most interesting, most extraordinary person in the universe." Then Emmet immediately adds, "And so is everybody." The reviewer noted this is part of a growing trend in corporate advertising: to mock the hype even as they engage in it.

I'm not saying that there is something wrong with moving to the city to pursue an adrenaline-racing calling. And I understand the fact that advertisers have always targeted our longing for self-importance. The real problem is that our values are changing and the new ones are wearing us out. But they're also keeping us from forming genuine, long-term, and meaningful commitments that actually contribute to the lives of others. Over time, the hype of living a new life, taking up a radical calling, and changing the world can creep into every area of our life. And it can make us tired, depressed, and mean.

Given the dominance of The Next Big Thing in our society, it is not at all surprising that the Christian subculture is passionate about superlatives. Many of us were raised in a Christian subculture of managed expectations, called to change ourselves or our world, with measurable results. There always had to be a cause du jour to justify our engagement. Otherwise, life in the church would simply be too ordinary. Like every other area of life, we have come to believe that growth in Christ—as individuals or as churches—can and should be programmed to generate predictable outcomes that are unrealistic and are not even justified biblically. We want big results—sooner rather than later. And we've forgotten that God showers his extraordinary gifts through ordinary means of grace, loves us through ordinary fellow image bearers, and sends us out into the world to love and serve others in ordinary callings.

Take, for example, the experience of Tish Harrison Warren. Raised in a wealthy evangelical church, sporting WWJD bracelets, she said, "I began to yearn for something more than a comfortable Christianity focused on saving souls and being generally respectable Republican Texans." Her story is typical of what many believers of her generation experienced—myself included:

> I was nearly 22 years old and had just returned to my college town from a part of Africa that had missed the last three centuries. As I walked to church in my weathered, worn-in Chaco's, I bumped into our new associate pastor and introduced myself. He smiled warmly and said, "Oh, you. I've heard about you. You're the radical who wants to give your life away for Jesus." It was meant as a compliment and I took it as one, but it also felt like a lot of pressure because, in a new way, I was torturously uncertain about what being a radical and living for Jesus was supposed to mean for me. Here I was, back in America, needing a job and health insurance, toying with dating this law student intellectual (who wasn't all that radical), and unsure about how to be faithful to Jesus in an ordinary life. I'm not sure I even knew if that was possible.

I entered college restless with questions and spent my twenties reading Marx and St. Francis, being discipled in the work of Rich Mullins, Ron Sider, and Tony Campolo, learning about New Monasticism (though it wasn't named that yet), and falling in love with Peter Maurin and Dorothy Day. My senior year of college, I invited everyone at our big student evangelical gathering to join me in protesting the School of the Americas.[3]

After spending time in various "radical" Christian communities, Warren began to wonder if ordinary life was even possible.

Now, I'm a thirty-something with two kids living a more or less ordinary life. And what I'm slowly realizing is that, for me, being in the house all day with a baby and a two-year-old is a lot more scary and a lot harder than being in a war-torn African village. What I need courage for is the ordinary, the daily every-dayness of life. Caring for a homeless kid is a lot more thrilling to me than listening well to the people in my home. Giving away clothes and seeking out edgy Christian communities requires less of me than being kind to my husband on an average Wednesday morning or calling my mother back when I don't feel like it.

"Everydayness Is My Problem"

Writer Rod Dreher observes, "Everydayness is my problem. It's easy to think about what you would do in wartime, or if a hurricane blows through, or if you spent a month in Paris, or if your guy wins the election, or if you won the lottery or bought that thing you really wanted. It's a lot more difficult to figure out how you're going to get through today without despair."[4] I know just how he feels. Even more than I'm afraid of failure, I'm *terrified* by boredom. Facing another day, with ordinary callings to ordinary people all around us is much more difficult than chasing my own dreams that I have envisioned for the grand story of my life. Other people—especially those closest to us—can become props. "The Poor" can be instruments of our life project. Or fighting "The Socialists" may animate our otherwise boring autobiography. Changing the world can be a way of actually avoiding the opportunities we have every day, right where God has placed us, to glorify and enjoy him and to enrich the lives of others.

It is all too easy to turn other people in our lives into a supporting cast for our life movie. The problem is that they don't follow the role or the lines we've given them. They are actual people with actual needs that get in the way of our plot, especially if they're as ambitious as we are. Sometimes, chasing your dreams can be "easier" than just being who we are, where God has placed you, with the gifts he has given to you.

American Christianity is a story of perpetual upheavals in churches and individual lives. Starting with the extraordinary conversion experience, our lives are motivated by a constant expectation for The Next Big Thing. We're growing bored with the ordinary means of God's grace, attending church week in and week out. Doctrines and disciplines that have shaped faithful Christian witness in the past are often marginalized or substituted with newer fashions or methods. The new and improved may dazzle us for the moment, but soon they have become "so last year."

In my own life so far, I've witnessed—and been part of—successive waves of enthusiasm that have whipped the church into a frenzy, only to leave many people exhausted or disillusioned. These fads change with every generation. So there are always fresh recruits to take the place of the burned-out enthusiasts of yesteryear. That, however, seems to be changing. For the first time, the percentage of American young adults claiming no religious affiliation has taken the lead (though barely) over those identifying themselves as evangelical Christians.

Aside from graduate school, I have spent my whole live in California. I lived a short drive from Azusa Street, the birthplace of Pentecostalism, and from Angelus Temple, where Sister Aimee Semple McPherson pioneered church-as-Vaudeville. Even closer were Calvary Chapel (the center of the "Jesus Movement" of the 1970s) and the Trinity Broadcasting Network (TBN) headquarters. Robert Schuller's Crystal Cathedral was just down the road, as was Saddleback Community Church, led by Pastor Rick Warren.

Thousands of pastors flocked to these venues regularly for church growth conferences.

Plagued by controversy, Sister Aimee Semple McPherson was caught up in an alleged kidnapping scandal. In the past several years, Calvary has suffered from various scandals, and it is unclear what shape its "Moses Model" of leadership will take after the recent death of its gifted founder Chuck Smith. "As one pastor said to *Christianity Today*, 'The Titanic has hit the iceberg. But the music is still playing.'"[5] Dedicated in the 1980s to "the glory of man, for the greater glory of God," the Crystal Cathedral declared bankruptcy in 2010 and two years later became Christ Cathedral, part of the Roman Catholic diocese of Orange County.[6]

Using the Crystal Cathedral as a prism, an article by Jim Hinch in *The American Scholar* observes that none of the trend-setting megachurches in Orange County is growing today.[7] Rob Bell, author of *Love Wins*, now calls Orange County home, but says that he surfs instead of going to church. "Evangelicals are good at whipping people up into a frenzy," he told Hinch, "and then you're like, 'What was that?'" The rapid growth in the county lies now with the largest Buddhist temple in the world (Itsi Lai) and the Islamic Society of Orange County. Recoiling from "McMansion" churches, many younger evangelicals are forming loose networks of "spiritual communities," Hinch reports. "In other words, the future of the evangelical church as glimpsed from Orange County might be no church at all."

The fads of the Boomer generation (those born between 1946 and 1964) were programs oriented around personal improvement and church growth. Boomers believed that traditional church experience was too ordinary—even boring—with its weekly routine of preaching, sacraments, prayer, praise, teaching, and fellowship. What was needed instead was a new plan for personal growth, something that would take our walk with God to "a whole new level." Boomers tended to make the Christian life—and the church—more individualistic and performance-oriented, removing checks and balances, structures and practices that have historically encouraged sustained growth in faith over the long haul.

Reacting against this self-focused and consumeristic approach, many of the children and grandchildren of the Boomer generation began looking outward, to problems in the world. The mantra swung from "change your life" to "change the world." Talk of evangelistic outreach shifted to calls for compassionate ministry to the poor, an emphasis on social justice, and an exhortation to live out your faith in a way that made a measurable difference in the world.

Yet both of these generational fads share something in common: *an impatience and disdain for the ordinary.* They share a passion for programs that deliver impressive, quick, and observable results. In both cases, the invitation is to break away from business-as-usual, to "think outside the box," and to do something big for God.

The tragedy in all of this is that something genuinely important in these calls is actually lost. We are called to grow in a personal relationship with Christ. We are also called to love and serve others—our fellow believers and our neighbors. And yet, the tendency of the evangelical movement has always been to prioritize extraordinary methods and demands over the ordinary means that Christ instituted for sustainable mission. Are we making it more difficult for the church to be a community where sinners are justified and renewed and are being conformed to Christ's image, bearing the fruit of good works for the good of their neighbors and the glory of God? Of course, it is true that God is doing great things through us. The real question is not *if* God will work through his people; rather, it's what we mean by "great" and how God has promised to do this work. What do people really mean when they talk about "changing the world"?

But I am convinced that we have drifted from the true focus of God's activity in this world. It is not to be found in the extraordinary, but in the ordinary, the everyday.

The problem is not that we are too active, but that we are recklessly frenetic. We have grown accustomed to quick fixes and easy solutions. We have grown accustomed to running sprints instead of training for the long-distance marathon. We have plenty of energy. The danger is that we will burn ourselves out on restless anxieties and unrealistic expectations.

To be clear, it's not as if all of the values being promoted today by calls to be "radical" or invitations to change the world are wrong-headed or unbiblical. Taking a summer to build wells in Africa is, for some, a genuine calling. But so is fixing a neighbor's plumbing, feeding one's family, and sharing in the burdens and joys of a local church. What we are called to do every day, right where God has placed us, is rich and rewarding.

Isn't This an Excuse to Be Comfortable?

When I return from spending time in the majority world, I'm convicted by the depth of my own addiction to comfort—having everything my way. Yet, there is a difference between an idol of comfort and genuine biblical contentment. Being content with life means accepting the circumstances in which God's providence has placed me. That can mean being content with poverty, if God so chooses. But it can also mean being content with my place as an average middle-class guy in an American suburb with a wife and four children—someone with various callings to my family, church, and neighborhood.

I never quite finished quoting from Tish Harrison Warren's provocative post. As she continues, she recalls a college friend who dedicated his life to teaching in the most at-risk schools. After a nervous breakdown, he moved back to his hometown, working as a waiter. Gradually, he recovered.

> When he'd landed back home, weary and discouraged, we talked about what had gone wrong. We had gone to a top college where people achieved big things. They wrote books and started non-profits. We were told again and again that we'd be world-changers. We were part of a young, Christian movement that encouraged us to live bold, meaningful lives of discipleship, which baptized this world-changing impetus as the way to really follow after Jesus. We were challenged to impact and serve the world in radical ways, but we never learned how to be an average person living an average life in a beautiful way.
>
> A prominent New Monasticism community house had a sign on the wall that famously read: "Everyone wants a revolution. No

one wants to do the dishes." My life is really rich in dirty dishes (and diapers) these days and really short in revolutions. I go to a church full of older people who live pretty normal, middle-class lives in nice, middle-class houses. But I have really come to appreciate this community, to see their lifetimes of sturdy faithfulness to Jesus, their commitment to prayer, and the tangible, beautiful generosity that they show those around them in unnoticed, unimpressive, unmarketable, unrevolutionary ways. And each week, we average sinners and boring saints gather around ordinary bread and wine and Christ himself is there with us.

She says that she still longs for a revolution and wants to make a difference in the wider world. She still disdains mediocrity.

But I've come to the point where I'm not sure anymore just what God counts as radical. And I suspect that for me, getting up and doing the dishes when I'm short on sleep and patience is far more costly and necessitates more of a revolution in my heart than some of the more outwardly risky ways I've lived in the past. And so this is what I need now: the courage to face an ordinary day—an afternoon with a colicky baby where I'm probably going to snap at my two-year old and get annoyed with my noisy neighbor—without despair, the bravery it takes to believe that a small life is still a meaningful life, and the grace to know that even when I've done nothing that is powerful or bold or even interesting that the Lord notices me and is fond of me and that that is enough.

The call to "radical discipleship," Warren notes, helpfully challenges our addiction to comfort. "But for those of us—and there are a lot of us—who are drawn to an edgy, sizzling spirituality, we need to embrace radical ordinariness and to be grounded in the challenge of the stable mundaneness of the well-lived Christian life." She concludes:

In our wedding ceremony, my pastor warned my husband that every so often, I would bound into the room, anxiety etched on my face, certain we'd settled for mediocrity because we weren't "giving our lives away" living in outer Mongolia. We laughed. All my radical friends laughed. And he was right. We've had that conversation many, many times. But I'm starting to learn that, whether in Mongolia or

Tennessee, the kind of "giving my life away" that counts starts with how I get up on a gray Tuesday morning. It never sells books. It won't be remembered. But it's what makes a life. And who knows? Maybe, at the end of days, a hurried prayer for an enemy, a passing kindness to a neighbor, or budget planning on a boring Thursday will be the revolution stories of God making all things new.[8]

Quantity Time

Think of the things that matter most to you. How do you measure your relationships? How do you "measure" your marriage, for example? When my wife and I talk about our relationship, we often have different takes on how things are going. Looking back over the course of our married years, we have seen many ways in which the Lord has bonded us together since our first year together. We can see steady growth and identify ways in which we've deepened in our relationship. But when we shift our focus to the short-term, the week-to-week, it becomes harder for us to get an accurate gauge on how we are doing. The extraordinary weekend retreat was memorable, but it's those ordinary moments filled with seemingly insignificant decisions, conversations, and touches that matter most. This is where most of life is lived. The richest things in life are made up of more than Kodak moments.

Is it any different when you are raising children? The mantra among many parents today, especially dads, is "Quality Time." But is that true? Think about all that happens in those mundane moments that are unplanned, unprogrammed, unscheduled, and unplugged. Nearly everything! Nicknames are invented, identities and relationships are formed. On the drive home from church, your child asks a question about the sermon that puts one more piece of the puzzle into place for an enduring faith. Everyone in the car benefits from the exchange.

I've used the "quality time" line before too, but it's just an excuse. Can we really compensate for extended absence (even if we are physically present), missing the ordinary details of life, with a dream getaway or by laying out a thousand dollars to take the kids to The

Wizarding World of Harry Potter? Any long-term relationship that wants to grow and be healthy needs those ordinary minutes, hours, days, months, and years. This is more than just enduring those moments passively. It requires engaging in intentional thought and effort as well as enjoyment. That's true also of our relationship with the triune God in his body, the visible church.

In the church today, we like to raise the bar, up the ante, and lay out radical calls that most people can't possibly answer. Nor do we expect them to, if we are honest. We understand that some will fly coach while others will find their way to first class. There are those dedicated few who are truly Spirit-filled, victorious, soul-winning, or society-transforming warriors. The rest of us are just "ordinary" believers. We will continue coming to church regularly, receiving God's gifts and sharing them, participating in praise, fellowship, and hospitality, and continue supporting the ministry financially. But we know, deep inside, that we aren't going to change the world.

None of this is new, of course. The same was true in the medieval church. It was fine to be an ordinary layperson, but everyone knew that if you wanted a direct route to a higher experience of God, you needed to be a priest or monk or nun. Marriage was good, but celibacy was seen as far better. Ordinary fellowship in the parish church and callings in the world were fine, but the truly dedicated took vows that set them apart from the ordinary Christian crowd. Some chose the monastic life, with other devoted colleagues. Others even more radically took a hermetic course of private isolation. Some made spiritual disciplines their focus, while others—especially the Franciscans—dedicated themselves to helping the poor.

We Protestants have our own way of programming various "higher" approaches to Christian living. Sure, you could still be a member of the local church, but if you've experienced the new birth you'll belong to the core—the true church that meets in small groups. They were often called "holy clubs" and "conventicles."

Then revivalism came along, sweeping aside external structures that helped to form individual believers into a thriving communion of saints. You may have been a beneficiary of God's covenant blessings over many years in a Christian family and church. But at the summer camp or revival meeting, none of this matters in comparison with the radical experience of conversion. Again, my point is not to downplay the thrill of conversion experiences. But we can come to expect jaw-dropping testimonies or novel experiences, and as a consequence we have created an environment of perpetual novelty.

You may be "saved," but are you "Spirit-filled"? You may have been baptized and looked after by Christ's under-shepherds in the church, joining gradually in the songs of Zion as you matured, and learning to join the church in its prayers and, eventually, at the Lord's Table. You may have heard and prayed the Scriptures with your family each day, perhaps even learning the great truths of Scripture through a catechism at home and at church. Yet in the evangelical culture of the new and novel, none of this really counts. What really matters is that extraordinary spiritual event, that life-changing experience. In fact, your testimony is likely to be regarded as greater—more genuine—to the extent that the experience happened apart from any connection with the ordinary life of the church, like baptism, profession, the Supper, and the communal prayers, praise, laments, and fellowship of Christ's body.

The problem is, when people enter adulthood, they soon discover that a memorable experience will not compensate for a shallow understanding of what they believe and why they believe it—over years of everyday exposure to and participation in the communion of Christ with his people. Nevertheless, it's precisely the ordinary ministry, week-in and week-out, that provides sustained growth and encourages the roots to grow deep. If the big moments in our Christian life are produced by big movements in the evangelical world, the ordinary local church will seem pretty irrelevant. Yet if God is the one who finishes what he starts, then the only reasonable conclusion is to be part of the garden that he is tending. He is the promise-maker and promise-keeper, even when we are unfaithful (2 Tim 2:13).

When she really wanted to single out a recent convert, my grandmother would say, "She wasn't just saved; she was *gloriously* saved." Reinforced by all the before-and-after conversion stories, I was pretty anxious over not having a great testimony, and I was tempted to embellish a little. After all, I couldn't even remember the date of the Big Moment! Unfortunately, it seemed, I was raised in a Christian home and church. I couldn't recall a time when I didn't trust in Christ and sense his gracious hand in my life. Here I was, basking in the benefits of Christ, growing in grace and knowledge of him. Yet I was always looking (and was expected to look for) a cataclysmic tsunami to wash all of that "churchianity" out to sea so that I could finally have a *real* relationship with Jesus.

I tried many of the programs offering a new experience, a new opportunity to grow and accomplish great things for God. I got saved several times (especially after watching "Thief in the Night" and reading Hal Lindsey's *The Late Great Planet Earth*). I dabbled in the charismatic movement, followed various "get-spiritual-quick" programs, did Evangelism Explosion, and for a while had a pastor who was drawn to the Shepherding Movement. I was drawn to the Christian Right, later the Christian Left, and by the time that the Church Growth Movement arrived on the scene, I was a little skeptical.

Then there was the emphasis on spiritual disciplines. Drawing on the contemplative tradition of medieval piety, this movement provoked many believers to take their personal walk with the Lord more seriously. There is a great deal of wisdom in this emphasis, particularly when we are distracted on every hand from the things that matter most. Still, it sometimes sounded simplistic and programmed: follow these steps and techniques and you will attain a victorious Christian life. The focus was on what we do alone more than on what God does for us and to us and through us together.

But even these personal disciplines can become too ordinary. What if Jesus actually spoke to you—apart from the words of Scripture? As Sarah Young tells us in the introduction to her runaway bestseller, *Jesus Calling*, "I knew that God communicated with me through the Bible, but I yearned for more. Increasingly, I wanted to hear what God had to say to me personally on a given day." That "more" was "the Presence of Jesus," something beyond the ordinary means of grace. "So I was ready to begin a new spiritual quest," beginning with Andrew Murray's *The*

Secret of the Abiding Presence. After reading *God Calling*, she relates, "I began to wonder if I, too, could receive messages during my times of communing with God." Even though Paul says that Christ's presence among us is "as near" as the word of Christ proclaimed (Rom 10:8–17), we long for something more.

In recent decades, the Emergent movement captured the attention of a generation, at least for a while. It promised another radical rebooting: "The Next Christians," "A New Kind of Christian," with the slogan, "Everything must change." Whenever a new generation announces its radical and totally unprecedented culture shift, there is an evangelical movement that pressures churches to get on board if they want to adapt and survive the next wave. It's doubtful that cultures actually work like that. But it is especially disruptive for the ordinary growth of believers in a covenant of grace that extends to every culture and "to a thousand generations." There is change, to be sure, but what kind of change, to what end, and through what means? For that, Scripture rather than culture must provide the ultimate answer.

Adapting to the culture—and especially to the profile of each generation—has been a remarkable strength of evangelicalism. Yet growing up into Christ as members of his body, across all generations and locales, is being undermined by frenetic relevance-operations. Patient dedication to the ordinary and often tedious disciplines of corporate and family worship, teaching, prayer, modeling, and mentoring have been eroded by successive waves of enthusiasm.

Even Calvinism seems to have gotten back its groove, taking its place on the "Next Big Thing" list. According to *Time* magazine in March 2009, the "New Calvinism" is one of the top ten trends changing the world today. Collin Hansen's movement-defining book sums it up pretty well: "Young, Restless, and Reformed."[9] But does this mean that it too is destined to become just another fad? It's the "restless" part that is problematic. It threatens to redefine what it means to be Reformed. Gifted leaders form movements. In a digital age, blogs are often more authoritative than sermons. But churches form confessions that live in the trenches that the Spirit digs and populates by his Word across all lands and generations. Joining a church, even a broader tradition, is not like joining a movement. Personal autonomy has to be surrendered to a communal consciousness of the triune God and his work in history. There is more to being Reformed than "five points."[10]

In many ways, it's more fun to be part of movements than churches. We can express our own individuality, pick our favorite leaders, and be swept off our feet at conferences. We can be anonymous. Although encouraged by like-minded believers, we are not bound up with them so that we should feel compelled to bear their burdens or suffer their rebukes. Yet this movement mentality keeps us restless and makes ordinary life in and submission to an actual church seem intolerably confining.

And terribly ordinary.

In all of these movements, something important was emphasized. Laypeople—including college students—enlisted cheerfully in the evangelistic cause. The call to spiritual disciplines reminded us that the Christian life is not simply a matter of assenting to propositions, but of a personal relationship with the Lord. Like any relationship, it has to be nurtured by daily attentiveness. It is also crucial to our faith that God is saving bodies, not just souls—and calls us to tangible service to others, especially the poor and marginalized in society. Yet the sustained attention of Christians over generations to these emphases is exactly what is at stake when each generation feels that it has to leave its distinctive mark.

For all of the interest in incorporating insights from the business world, many church leaders seem to have missed the suggestion of Thomas J. Peters and Nancy K. Austin in their best-selling *A Passion for Excellence* back in 1985:

> So a revolution is brewing. What kind of revolution? In large measure it is in fact a "back to basics" revolution. The management systems, schemes, devices and structures, promoted during the last quarter century, have added up to distractions from the main ideas: the achievement of sustainable growth and equity. Each such scheme seemed to make sense at the time. Each seemed an appropriate response to growing complexity. But the result was that the

basics got lost in a blur of well-meaning gibberish that took us further and further from excellent performance in any sphere.[11]

We need to recover not only sound doctrine, but sounder practices that serve to deepen us—and succeeding generations—in the new creation that God has called into being. We need to question not only false teaching, but false values, expectations, and habits that we have absorbed, taken for granted, and even adopted with a veneer of piety. Despite the touching sentimentality of my grandmother's favorite hymn, "In the Garden," it is simply not true that you come to the garden alone with Jesus and "the joy we share as we tarry there none other has ever known." If your personal relationship with Jesus is utterly unique, then it is not properly Christian.

Though a proposed cure requires a diagnosis, this book is not primarily a critique. In the first place, I write as someone who suffers with the illnesses I'm trying to understand and treat. Furthermore, I don't have anybody particularly in mind.

This book is dedicated to all of the pastors, elders, and deacons whose service is as unheralded as it is vital to sustainable discipleship; to all of the spouses and parents who cherish ordinary moments to love and be loved, and to all of those believers who consider their ordinary vocations in the world as part of God's normal way of loving and serving neighbors right under their nose each day.

And who knows? Maybe if we discover the opportunities of the ordinary, a fondness for the familiar, and marvel again at the mundane, we will be radical after all.

Exercise

1. What are some examples of ways in which you feel the pull toward the "radical" as opposed to the ordinary? Consider/ discuss various movements, trends, and programs you've encountered that seemed to grab your allegiance and then dissipate.

2. Do you have a problem with "everydayness"? How does the Christian subculture sometimes contribute to this?

CHAPTER 2

ordinary isn't mediocre

I can already see the objections forming in your mind. *If people cherished the ordinary, there would not only be no Steve Jobs, no Wright Brothers, no Martin Luther King Jr; there wouldn't have been church fathers and mothers, reformers, and pioneering missionaries. This call to embrace the ordinary sounds biblical, but aren't you really asking people to settle for less? To give up their dreams?*

I realize that this is the conclusion some will draw from reading the title of this book, so I want to offer a response: ordinary does not mean mediocre.

In fact, far from throwing a wet blanket on godly passion, my goal is to encourage an orientation and habits that foster deeper growth in grace, more effective outreach, and a more sustainable vision of loving service to others over a lifetime. This is not a call to do less, but to invest in things that we often give up on when we don't see an immediate return. The fact that "ordinary" has come to mean mediocre and low expectations is a sign of the problem I want to address.

The Warping of Excellence

There are no shortcuts to excellence in any area of life, and it is commitment to the ordinary that makes the difference.

Many of us had parents who were the wind beneath our wings. They encouraged us to aim for the stars. Maybe you can recall a coach or teacher who believed in you when you weren't so sure of yourself. People like that are worth their weight in gold. I'm all for reading *The Little Engine That Could* to your kids, and I admire the immigrants who work their fingers to the bone to make a better life with better opportunities for their children. We cannot live without drives, passions, and goals. God wired us this way and he pronounced it "good."

Yet everything that the Bible identifies as sin and our nature recognizes as such is *something essentially good gone wrong*. More precisely, it is something God has made that we have corrupted. Augustine defined the essence of sin as being *curved in on ourselves*. Instead of looking up to God in faith and out to our neighbors in love, we turn inward. We use God's good gifts as weapons in the service of our mutiny against him and each other. We can even use spiritual programs to perpetuate this narcissism.

Excellence is going over and beyond the call of duty. But to what end? More than anything else, excellence demands a worthy object and a worthy goal. We have this worthy object: "The chief end of man is to glorify God and to enjoy him forever," begins the Westminster Shorter Catechism. The call to excellence is useless by itself. We can no more stir up a passion for excellence than we can will a passion for love. It is only by discovering a worthy object of desire that we find ourselves interested in pursuing it.

Excellence requires caring about someone or something enough to invest time, effort, and skill into it, with God's glory and our neighbor's good as the goal. Biblically defined, true excellence has *others* in mind—first God, and then our neighbor. "So, whether you eat or drink, or whatever you do, do all to the glory of God" (1 Cor 10:31). Eating and drinking are fairly common aspects of daily life, and yet even ordinary meals become significant when they draw our attention once again to glorifying and enjoying the God who provides them.

The warping of excellence occurs when we believe "it's all about us." The clumsy kid will only be able to play at a higher level for the varsity basketball team when the game becomes the focus, not his performance. He has to get over himself and the misgivings he felt and just be part of the team. Or consider a musician. Instead of just playing the music, one may become too busy admiring or criticizing his or her performance. When this happens, "standards of excellence" we've created—at school, at work, in the church, and in family life—can easily become an idol. We project a certain image of ourselves or of the persona we would like to project, and we guard it at all costs. Literally and figuratively, we've taken our eyes off the ball.

Obviously, excellence is not the problem; we are. The question is whether by excellence we mean quality or quantity, hype or substance, perpetual novelty or maturity. If we were to measure excellence by God's standards, the list might seem a little strange: "love, joy, peace, patience, kindness, goodness, faithfulness, gentleness, self-control" (Gal 5:22). Not exactly the qualities that are mentioned in job postings for leaders these days. I have to say—and it will not come as a surprise to anyone involved in ministry—things seem little different in the church.

There are moments in church history, and in our own church experience, when divisions occur over doctrinal issues. However, our churches, our marriages, and our lives are threatened more by a failure to cultivate this fruit of the Spirit. Love, joy, peace, and patience are the fruit of that faith given to us by the Spirit through the gospel. Yet, ironically, the calls to be radical and extraordinary may cut off such fruit at its root. Instead of arising as the fruit of our union with Christ, these qualities become a way of separating the sheep from the goats—or at least the prize-winning sheep from the rest of the flock.

This ungodly sort of ambition can take a variety of forms. Tribes gather around a charismatic figure, and then the movement exalts itself over other churches or movements that haven't caught up with the "new thing" that God is doing. Patience is precisely what excellence requires, but it's a difficult commodity wherever the cult of immediate results dominates. Faithfulness over the long haul is undermined by perpetual innovation.

In more conservative churches, love, joy, peace, and patience may be thwarted by a censorious temperament that's always poised to pounce. And faithfulness may be avoided by a refusal to accept necessary reforms in the light of God's Word. It is all too easy to assert our own list of orthodoxies and rules as "something more" than what God has revealed in his Word. It is easier to alienate than to teach with humility and love. We too quickly write people off, in contrast to the Good Shepherd, who does not break off a bruised reed or quench a faintly burning candle. Epithets of "fundamentalist" and "liberal" ricochet around us in reckless shots.

In either case, we are not finding our common source in the gospel, nor do we restrict the expectations of Christ's way of life to what is actually commanded in Scripture. Instead, we invent our own ideals of "missional living" and "radical discipleship" or our own list of doctrinal essentials and then impose them on God's people as necessary for faith and life. As a result, the mature qualities of gentleness and self-control become subordinate, at least in practice, to the sort of visceral and often ill-informed judgments that we once associated with adolescence.

My point is that these qualities — the "fruit of the Spirit" — are cultivated in the fertile soil of the gospel; they wither in the toxic atmosphere of restless innovation as well as sleepy traditionalism.

You pursue excellence when you care about something other than your own excellence. You find yourself desiring something or someone whose inherent truth, beauty, and goodness draw you in. You love a particular object enough to endure whatever setbacks and challenges stand in your way. That's true of anyone who is driven by a worthy prospect, romance, cause, or calling.

A World War II aircraft mechanic, my father was also an expert carpenter, plumber, and electrician. On that score, absolutely none of his genetic material was passed down to me. The apple fell very, very far from the tree, rolled down a busy intersection, and was crushed by a truck. When my father gave me a job, I pursued it halfheartedly and usually left it half done. It was only as I grew older that I was able to care more about these tasks, and I did so because they mattered to my dad.

While we cannot care about everything equally at the same time, mediocrity results from not caring at all. Mediocrity is as likely with rushed cathedral building as it is with lazy apathy. If shortsighted bursts of enthusiasm fail to provide sustainable growth, excellence is threatened also by a conservatism that settles for the status quo. In countless examples of those we consider successful in life we can see there was a patient commitment to daily routines, routines that to the outside observer seem dull, trivial, worthless. We may admire Mother Theresa and her daily commitment to the poor, but we'd rather win the lottery.

Consider the Cologne Cathedral. Begun in 1248, the Gothic jewel was to be the main place of worship for the Holy Roman emperors. Frederick II knew he would not see its completion. Consistent building continued until 1473. Halted during the sixteenth century, the construction was completed in 1880 according to the original plan—632 years after the turn of the first shovel. Towering above the city skyline to this day, the building owes its overwhelming grandeur to its meticulous design and execution over centuries. Even with modern engineering and materials, it would be impossible to duplicate the Cologne Cathedral. It was what *Good to Great* author Jim Collins would call a "big, hairy, audacious goal." Yet its completion depended on the patient skill of countless individuals who knew that they would probably never see the ribbon-cutting ceremony.

So how do we want to grow? Well, it all depends on what it is and why we care about it in the first place. McDonalds and the Cologne Cathedral reflect different objects, ends, and means—and therefore, different definitions of excellence. It's hard to contest the excellence with which the fast-food company fulfills the mission statement on its website:

> McDonald's brand mission is to be our customers' favorite place and way to eat and drink. Our worldwide operations are aligned around a global strategy called the Plan to Win, which centers on an exceptional customer experience—People, Products, Place, Price and Promotion. We are committed to continuously improving our operations and enhancing our customers' experience.

But that definition of excellence would never have led to the building of the Cologne Cathedral. The fruit of excellence is determined by the object. Only the worthiness of the object can sustain long-term excellence.

Jesus Christ also had a "big, hairy, audacious goal." In his case, the outcome was certain. Grounded in the covenant made between the persons of the Trinity before the foundation of the world, the Son was given a people. As their mediator, he became flesh to redeem them from the condition into which they had plunged themselves. Upon ascending to the place of all authority, he and his Father sent the Spirit to gather his people from every tribe into one holy nation. And on the basis of this authority that he has won he gave his apostles the mission statement: "Go therefore and make disciples of all nations, baptizing them in the name of the Father and of the Son and of the Holy Spirit, teaching them to observe all that I have commanded you" (Matt 28:19–20).

We may be discouraged by circumstances on the ground, in our own churches and denominations. Nevertheless, there can be no doubt that Christ's "little flock" centered in Jerusalem has now spread into every part of the world. Even in the face of perennial persecution from without and corruption from within, the church is still the kingdom that Christ is building, with himself as the cornerstone. In addition to the church's mission, believers have their various callings in the communion of saints and also as parents and children, carpenters and doctors, friends and neighbors, volunteers and citizens. Some are called to positions of leadership in the City of God and the City of Man, while others play humbler but no less important roles. In either case, we are all called to excellence, according to the criteria appropriate to each calling's object and aim.

Some people choose an object to pursue, but they lack the commitment to sustain growth. Again, this depends on how badly you want it—in other words, how desirable the object is to you. You may want to lose weight or get in shape, but a successful athlete knows that it's not the sudden bursts, energy drinks, and new-and-improved training video that leads to success; it's the countless minutes and hours logged in the gym. If I walk into the gym and tell a good trainer, "Hey, I'd like to have six-pack abs in three weeks," he'll tell me (if he's honest) that I'm setting myself up for failure. Yet the advertisements still sell us on the unrealistic promise, and we fall for it.

Rosa Parks didn't wake up one day and decide to become the "First Lady of Civil Rights." She just boarded the bus as she did every day for work and decided that this day she wasn't going to sit in the back as a proper black person was expected to do in 1950s Montgomery, Alabama. She knew who she was and what she wanted. She knew the cost, and she made the decision to pursue what she believed in enough to sacrifice her own security. At that point, she wasn't even joining a movement. She was just the right person at the right place and time. What made her the right person were countless influences, relation-ships, and experiences—most of them seemingly insignificant and forgotten. God had already shaped her into the sort of person who would do such a thing. For her at least, it was an ordinary thing to refuse to sit in the back of the bus on this particular trip. But for his-tory, it had radical repercussions.

People who actually know what the eventual cost might be and how little change you see quickly are more likely to counsel patience. But we believe the ads. We think we can become a connoisseur of fine wines with a kit, learn to build a patio by watching YouTube clips, or master a new language with a set of CDs while driving to work. But real growth, the cultivation of excellence, doesn't work like that. The key is a loving, patient, attentive care to the things that really matter—things that we're likely to ignore in our overachieving rush to relevance and radical impact. Excellence means that whether God calls me to serve the poor in Calcutta or diners in a French restaurant, the simple fact that it is God's calling renders it precious. "So ... whatever you do, do all to the glory of God" (1 Cor 10:31).

Excellence cannot be cultivated by lone rangers. We may remem-ber some of the great scientists, artists, and philanthropists in his-tory. But they would never have acquired their knowledge or skills apart from being formed by a community of expertise over time.

Standards of excellence in each of these fields are not something that each person invents or even votes on. Rather, they evolve over generations through countless negotiations, failures, and successes.

This is why Christ places us in a local expression of his visible body. Especially as Americans we think that we can figure things out on our own. We are only a "do-it-yourself" guide, seminar, or mouse click away from mastering whatever we want to do or be. However, in any field, excellence requires discipline — submitting to a community that cultivates expertise. Discipline requires disciples, just as craftsmanship requires apprentices. Much wisdom for this discipleship may be found in the community's accumulated resources. However, books will not be sufficient. In the church today, we do not need more conferences, more programs, and more celebrities. We need more churches where the Spirit is immersing sinners into Christ day by day, a living communion of the saints, where we cannot simply jump to our favorite chapter or Google our momentary interest.

Excellence versus Perfectionism

Excellence is a virtue when it has God's glory and our neighbor's good in view. Yet, as with all virtues, self-love turns this noble drive into a vice. It can take many forms. One of them is perfectionism.

In the case of aspiring perfectionists, the craving for approval can paralyze them from receiving God's mercy and serving their neighbors in simple — and imperfect — ways. Eventually, many in this class acknowledge defeat and curl up inside themselves. "I'll never do *that* again!" they say to themselves. The desire to please others — to derive their identity from the words of someone other than God — has a debilitating effect on their hearts. Instead of living *from* God's justification of the ungodly in Christ, they live *for* the approval and applause of other sinners. When that approval is lacking, they close up, pull away, and retreat from the world — and perhaps even God. The fear of failing, the fear of rejection, and the desire to avoid pain keep them from pursuing excellence in a healthy way that honors God.

In the case of deluded perfectionists, success has the opposite effect:

to intoxicate them with the illusion of self-justification. It can become a terrible drug. Rather than placing our trust in God, we learn to trust in our own piety and devotion. Our tireless service is driven more by a desire for self-justification and self-acclaim than by being secure in Christ enough to tend now to the actual needs of others.

When I find my justification in Christ alone, I am free to love and serve others in ordinary and unheralded ways. A relatively insignificant and imperfect act of generosity is nevertheless useful to my neighbor and therefore glorifying to God. Our perfectionism, however, makes others and their needs simply an instrument for loving and serving ourselves. We might have a so-called "messiah" complex, and this insatiable need within us drives us to do things that will make us well-eulogized in the end. We want to have "an excellent life" inscribed on our tombstone and prove that we are people of worth and value.

Sadly, even something simple like a desire to serve by hosting a lovely dinner can become warped by our desire to impress. Soon, it is no longer the pleasure of the guests, but their acclaim that makes it all worth the effort. If I place great importance on their acclaim, I will spare no expense and go to extravagant lengths to ensure their approval. By contrast, true excellence—done out of love for others to the glory of God, from faith in Christ—can involve nothing more than having an extra plate for stew in case someone drops in.

This is precisely what Jesus encountered one Sabbath as he was invited to dine with distinguished guests at the home of a leader of the Pharisees. At first glance, this episode ranks as an egregious example of social recklessness on the part of Jesus. After raising eyebrows over healing a man on the Sabbath, Jesus turns their thinly veiled attack (with the generic question, "Is it lawful to heal on the Sabbath, or not?") into a sermon on hospitality. He reveals that the religious leaders weren't really interested in excellence, at least not the kind that is done from faith and in service to love for one's neighbor. For them, excellence had to do with measuring up to moral rules that they had invented. In their idolatry of legalistic excellence, they missed an opportunity to be saved—from themselves.

Jesus turns the tables on them and lectures them on proper dinner etiquette in his kingdom. He begins with the seating arrangement: "When you are invited by someone to a wedding feast, do not sit down in a place of honor, lest someone more distinguished than you be invited by him.... For everyone who exalts himself will be humbled, and he who humbles himself will be exalted" (Luke 14:8 – 11). In essence, don't wait for the host to move you to the children's table.

Jesus is not giving general lessons in dining etiquette. He is calling the sinners and outcasts to his feast, while the religious leaders who refused his generosity were left out in the cold. He is the host at this meal, not the guest. And if they do not let themselves be served at his table—along with the other sinners off the street, they will go hungry. In any case, they are in for some surprises if they think that they have the place of honor at his table.

Jesus even gives his host a warning in the form of a parable about a wedding banquet. "When you give a dinner or banquet, do not invite your friends or your brothers or your relatives or rich neighbors, lest they also invite you in return and you be repaid." At first, this doesn't make any sense: "*lest* they also invite you in return and you be repaid"? Isn't this the simple law of hospitality? If you throw a nice party for people, it is likely that you will be rewarded with invitations from them? But that's not what Jesus tells them. "But when you give a feast," he continues, "invite the poor, the crippled, the lame, the blind, and you will be blessed, because they cannot repay you" (Luke 14:12 – 14). Jesus tells the religious leaders that they should invite the very people whom they excluded from the precincts of the temple. These leaders were likely confused. After all, these sordid characters were excluded so that the excellence and purity of the temple could be preserved. Why would *they* be invited to the feast?

To cut the parable short, Jesus has the host of the great banquet send servants out to invite people to the feast. One by one, the engraved invitations are graciously declined. If you define excellence in self-centered terms, they are declined for good reasons. Finally, the master sends his servant out to the alleys: Go out to the alleys, he says, "and compel people to come in, that my house may be filled. For I tell you, none of those men who were invited shall taste my banquet" (Luke 14:15–24).

On the heels of this episode, Luke inserts Jesus' instruction to the crowds on the cost of discipleship, concluding: "So therefore, any one of you who does not renounce all that he has cannot be my disciple" (Luke 14:33). This is not an abstract warning, much less a proof text for a monastic vow of poverty. What Jesus is saying is that every excuse for refusing the master's invitation—even the pursuit of religious "excellence"—will make you an outsider to his kingdom. Your religious excellence will not earn you a place at God's table. Your own efforts will never merit you a seat of honor. The invitation is not Christ plus anything, but Christ alone. Material, moral, or spiritual self-sufficiency is deadly, and it has everlasting consequences.

Everything that Jesus is saying in this parable he is fulfilling in their midst. He is spreading the table and inviting his guests. As it turns out, the religious insiders are really the outsiders and the outsiders—those rejected from the temple life—are now made insiders through faith in Christ. When we turn a godly passion for excellence (that is, glorifying and enjoying God and loving our neighbors) into an idol of our own self-justification, we miss the truly radical thing that God is doing right under our noses.

Being "ordinary" means that we reject the idolatry of pursuing excellence for selfish reasons. We aren't digging wells in Africa to prove our worth or value. We aren't serving in the soup kitchen or engaging in spiritual disciplines because we long to be unique, radical, and different. When we do these things for selfish reasons, God becomes a tool for winning our lifetime achievement award. Our neighbors become instruments in the crafting of our sense of meaning, impact, and identity. What we do for God is really for ourselves.

Instead, our affections must be realigned and our priorities reordered. Jesus Christ fulfilled all righteousness during his thirty-plus years of perfect obedience to all that the Father had commanded. He did that for us. Having done the work that we were supposed to do, he bore the sentence of divine justice and paid the debt we had piled up. He is now raised, sitting at the Father's right hand, interceding for us. Here, before the face of the exalted Savior, we behold the portrait of true excellence. He alone is the unique substitute—the guilt offering by his death, so that now we can be not only forgiven but offer up ourselves as "living sacrifices" of praise and thanksgiving (Rom 12:1). It is admittedly paradoxical: only by resting in Christ do we find ourselves active in good works, not just for the sprints but for the long-distance run.

The Call to Action

The call to action, to have an active faith, is well-supported in Scripture. "Ordinary" does not mean passive. All believers should live out what they believe, should practice what they preach. But misguided or chaotic activism makes us sloppy. The real question is: What kind of action? Why—and to what end? There is a difference between frenetic activism and faithful activity in the daily struggles and joys of life.

Some, in defending the doctrine of "grace alone," have given the impression that there is nothing we need to do as a Christian. It is certainly true that there is nothing that we can do to be righteous in God's courtroom. How do you qualify for the mercy and forgiveness of a holy God? By being a transgressor of his law. (In other words, we all qualify.)

Nor can we do anything to raise ourselves from spiritual death. The new birth is a gift. Not even our faith causes this new birth. In any case, faith is not something we possess, our contribution to the enterprise; it is the gift of God (Eph 2:8–9). Calls to action cannot assume the gospel. Otherwise, the church itself—even in the name of evangelism—conspires with the world in driving us deeper into ourselves.

The power of our activism, campaigns, movements, and strategies cannot forgive sins or raise the dead. "The gospel … is the power of God for salvation," and, with Paul, we have no reason to be ashamed of it (Rom 1:16). That is why phrases like "living the gospel," "being the gospel," and "being partners with Jesus in his redemption of the world" are dangerous distortions of the biblical message of good news. The gospel is not about what we have done or are called to do, but the announcement of God's saving work in Jesus Christ. "For what we proclaim is not ourselves, but Jesus Christ as Lord, with ourselves as your servants for Jesus' sake" (2 Cor 4:5).

So first and foremost—and always—we are recipients before God. He is the benefactor and we are the beneficiaries. We cannot give him anything he needs, but we receive everything from his hand (Acts 17:25; Rom 11:35–36; Jas 1:17). The gospel is not a warm-up for the lightning round of our schemes of self-improvement and world transformation. We need to hear the good news each day.

However, the whole point of the gospel is to raise the dead, to justify the ungodly, to transform and liberate us to glorify and enjoy God and to love and serve our neighbors! Chosen, justified, and adopted by the Father, in the Son, we are united to Christ by the Spirit through the gift of faith. This is the same Holy Spirit who separated the waters in creation and in the exodus, for the safe passage of his covenant people to the holy land; the same one who filled the temple; the same one who made the eternal Son incarnate in the womb of a virgin, led and sustained him through his earthly trial, empowered him to perform wonders, and raised him from the dead.

This same Holy Spirit has not only given us new birth, uniting us to our living Head; he has taken up residence within us. His indwelling makes us holy, just as it once had made the temple and the whole land of Israel holy. Unlike the temple, the Spirit's indwelling presence in his saints cannot be withdrawn. His residence is the security deposit on our final redemption (Rom 8:23). Meditate on these words:

> If the Spirit of him who raised Jesus from the dead dwells in you, he who raised Christ Jesus from the dead will also give life to your mortal bodies through his Spirit who dwells in you.
>
> So then, brothers, we are debtors, not to the flesh, to live according to the flesh.... For you did not receive the spirit of slavery to

fall back into fear, but you have received the Spirit of adoption as sons, by whom we cry, "Abba! Father!" (Rom 8:11 – 15)

We are still sinful, but we are no longer "dead in ... trespasses and sins" (Eph 2:1). And although, in the act of justification, faith is merely resting in Christ and receiving him with all of his gifts, this same faith clings to Christ also for sanctification. The Spirit creates faith through the gospel and saving faith bears the fruit of love and good works. We are united to Christ for justification *and* renewal. These must be distinguished, but never separated. Saving faith is not the enemy of good works, but their only possible source.

Before God, we are always receivers of gifts. Before our neighbors, however, we are both receivers and givers. Even our praise is offered up as a sacrifice of thanksgiving, not as an atoning sacrifice. It is in view of God's mercies, not in the hope of attaining them, that we offer our bodies as living sacrifices (Rom 12:1 – 2). As Luther said, "God does not need our good works; our neighbor does."[12] Calvin says the same thing in discussing the exchange of gifts in the body of Christ. "Since our good deeds cannot reach God anyway, he gives us instead other believers unto whom we can do good deeds. The one who wants to love God can do so by loving the believers."[13]

We never offer up our good works to God for salvation, but extend them to our neighbors for their good. As a result, everyone benefits. God, who needs nothing from us, receives all of the glory; our neighbors receive gifts that God wants to give them through us; and we benefit both from the gifts of others and the joy that our own giving brings. Reverse this flow, and nobody wins. God is not glorified, neighbors are not served, and we live frustrated, anxious, joyless lives awaiting the wrath of a holy God.

The gospel produces peace and empowers us to live by faith. We are no longer anxious, but secure and invigorated because we are crucified and raised with Christ. We are no longer trying to live up to the starring role we've given ourselves, but are written into the story of Christ. We have nothing to prove, just a lot of work to do. Good works are no longer seen as a condition of our union with Christ, but as its fruit. We are no longer slaves, but the children of

God—co-heirs with Christ, our elder brother. The first question and answer of the Heidelberg Catechism summarizes this faith well:

> Q. What is your only comfort in life and in death?
> A. That I am not my own,
>   but belong—
>   body and soul,
>   in life and in death—
>   to my faithful Savior, Jesus Christ.
>   He has fully paid for all my sins with his precious blood,
>   and has set me free from the tyranny of the devil.
>   He also watches over me in such a way
>   that not a hair can fall from my head
>   without the will of my Father in heaven;
>   in fact, all things must work together for my salvation.
>   Because I belong to him,
>   Christ, by his Holy Spirit,
>   assures me of eternal life
>   and makes me wholeheartedly willing and ready
>   from now on to live for him.[14]

As God's creatures, made in his image, we are "not our own" already in creation. Yet our redemption doubles this truth. Created by God and saved by his grace, I am truly "not my own, but belong—body and soul, in life and in death—to my faithful Savior, Jesus Christ."

Toward the end of the Heidelberg Catechism (after treating the Ten Commandments), the question is asked, "But can those converted to God obey these commandments perfectly?" I love the answer: "No. In this life even the holiest have only a small beginning of this obedience. Nevertheless, with all seriousness of purpose, they do begin to live according to all, not only some, of God's commandments."[15] Notice we are not looking for a balance between passivity and perfectionism. Both are rejected. In his own experience, Paul laments that even when he sins, he is still loving the law and its Giver (Rom 7:14–25). It is precisely this quandary that makes the Christian life such a struggle.

It is with this confidence that we can embrace the exhortations in Scripture to press on, to grow in knowledge and maturity, to keep up with the Spirit rather than grieve him, and to offer our bodies to righteousness and put to death the deeds of our sinful nature. Instead of mounting up to heaven in self-righteous ambition, we reach out to those who are right under our nose each day who need something that we have to offer. Christ is our rock. And when we fall off, we get back on that rock, secure in the identity that he has given us, and we keep striving to distribute his loving gifts to others.

When we come to passages that call us to live in a manner that is pleasing to the Lord, we are meant to hear them as those who have already been justified as adopted heirs. The same command can inspire terror or delight, depending on whether the one who commands is our Father or our Judge. We cannot please God as a Judge, but we can please him as our Father. We cannot offer any sacrifice for our guilt — a sacrilege after the Lamb of God has been slain once and for all. His atoning sacrifice frees us now to offer our bodies as "a living sacrifice" of praise and thanksgiving (Rom 12:1; Phil 4:18; Heb 13:16; 1 Pet 2:5).

Since our failures are liberally pardoned by a merciful Father in Christ, we can strive "to walk in a manner worthy of the Lord, fully pleasing to him, bearing fruit in every good work and increasing in the knowledge of God." We are not motivated by fear of rejection or a need to seek approval. Instead, it is a life of "endurance and patience with joy, giving thanks to the Father, who has qualified [us] to share in the inheritance of the saints in light." Why? "He has delivered us from the domain of darkness and transferred us to the kingdom of his beloved Son, in whom we have redemption, the forgiveness of sins" (Col 1:10 – 14).

It is a life no longer turned in on ourselves, alternating between despair and pride, but of putting the spotlight on Christ for his glory and as a witness to those outside whom he will make co-heirs with us in the inheritance. So whether we live or die, Paul says, "we make it our aim to please him" (2 Cor 5:9).

So here's some relief to perfectionists out there: Give up! Stop climbing and fall into God's gracious arms. "For you have died, and your life is hidden with Christ in God" (Col 3:3). Awakened by a true understanding of God's law and your own life, you'll never be a perfectionist again, at least in principle. (Getting used to it is a different matter.) So get on with life, with love, with service—fully realizing that God already has the perfect service he requires of us in his Son and now our neighbor needs our imperfect help. Now, with confidence in the gospel, use God's law as a guide rather than as a means of self-justification. Precisely because we cling to Christ alone for our peace with God, we are liberated to love and serve others without trying to score points.

And notice that all of the Ten Commandments are oriented toward others: God and neighbor. Much of our piety is focused on "me and my inner life." Just look at the Christian Living section of the average Christian bookstore. Yet God's commands are focused on what it means to be in a relationship with others: to trust in God alone and to love and worship him in the way he approves and to look out for the good of our fellow image bearers.

On the heels of the question and answer above, the Heidelberg Catechism asks, "Since no one in this life can obey the Ten Commandments perfectly, why does God want them preached so pointedly?" Answer: "First, so that the longer we live the more we may come to know our sinfulness and the more eagerly look to Christ for forgiveness of sins and righteousness." Even in the Christian life we need this first use of the law to drive us out of ourselves to cling to our Savior. "Second, so that we may never stop striving, and never stop praying to God for the grace of the Holy Spirit, to be renewed more and more after God's image, until after this life we reach our goal: perfection."[16]

"Because of Christ alone, embraced through faith alone, for the glory of God and the good of our neighbors alone, on the basis of God's Word alone"—and nothing more. This is the slogan of the ordinary Christian (Luke 10:27).

Exercise

1. What is excellence?
2. How do we turn this virtue into a vice? Think/talk about the difference between excellence and perfectionism.
3. Is the call to embrace the ordinary a cop-out for mediocrity?
4. Is it a call to passivity? If not, what is the rationale for activity as Christians?

the young and the restless

We're all adolescents now," writes Thomas Bergler. "When are we going to grow up?"[17] Bergler explains that churches and parachurch organizations first began to provide youth-oriented programs—mainly to help at-risk kids in the cities (e.g., the YMCA). Then the "teenager" was invented as a unique demographic in society. As a result, the youth group was created, offering adolescent-friendly versions of church. "In the second stage, a new adulthood emerged that looked a lot like the old adolescence. Fewer and fewer people outgrew the adolescent Christian spiritualities they had learned in youth groups; instead, churches began to cater to them." Eventually, churches *became* them.[18]

It is nothing new when young people want churches to pander to them. What is new is the extent to which churches have obliged. In previous generations, elders—both officers and simply older and wiser members—wouldn't let that happen. They took young people under their wing and taught them by word and example what it meant to begin to accept the privileges and responsibilities of membership in Christ's body. The youth were not a market to exploit, but lambs to feed and guard. Churches saw young people neither as the measure of their success nor as "the church of tomorrow," but as an integral part of the church today.

For the first time in the history of the church, it has become possible to go from the nursery to children's church to Sunday school to the youth group and college ministry without ever actually having experienced church membership. Shocking surveys abound reporting that many of our children are dropping out of church by their college years. But maybe it shouldn't be so shocking if they were never actually involved in church to begin with.

Increasingly I meet young pastors who never, or rarely, experienced the ordinary means of grace in the weekly service. Some were never baptized, much less instructed in a common catechism in preparation for making profession and coming to Holy Communion. Unfortunately, the people I have in mind were not adult converts, but belonged to a Christian family and attended countless Christian events and ministries sponsored by the church. The whole plan of gradual maturity in Christ's body was set aside for perpetual adolescence. Their whole world was a youth culture. Many were raised more by their peers than by their parents and pastors. And today many are themselves both.

So it's not surprising perhaps that, like the culture generally, many churches deemed most "alive" and "cutting-edge" reflect a near obsession with youth. My mentor, James Montgomery Boice, used to say that instead of the more biblical pattern of children growing toward maturity, churches were turning adults into children. Positively, this youthful orientation provided energy and zeal, but it also changed our spiritual ecology.

Young *Is* Restless

With good reason—and ageless experience—we associate childhood with a spirit of restless exploration, wonder, and distraction. These characteristics may create frustration at times, but we do not normally associate them with vice. Fascinated by the newness of everything, their attention shifts back and forth, up and down. We greet crawling and then walking with short-lived joy, as the dear ones pull every pot out of the cupboard and wander away from us at the supermarket. They have not yet learned how to anticipate danger or to discern the important from the trivial; *everything* is interesting! Thus, they can be more easily exploited and even abused.

Children are trusting. But if they stay that way, they're gullible.

As children, we did not take time to chew properly, much less to meditate deeply on truth. We ask, "Are we there yet?" twenty minutes after leaving our driveway. We do not expect infants to take care of others, to consider others as more important than themselves. We do not scold five-year-olds for failing to find work. It's the brief and shining moment in life when the spotlight was on us and our needs, without any expectation that it should be otherwise.

As we mature, expectations change. But, like learning to ride a bike, it's basically trial and error. The most exasperating aspect of taking my children fishing is that they won't leave the line in the water long enough to attract a living thing. Yes, this sort of impatience is childish—which is perfectly normal in a child. Carried into adulthood, though, it is aggravating.

Growing Up

We're called to enter the kingdom like children (Matt 18:3; Luke 18:16), but not to remain locked in the perpetual restlessness of childhood and adolescence. Eventually we learn to make commitments, develop roots, and invest our lives in long-term relationships instead of constantly searching for the newest, greatest, and latest. Through their ministry, pastors-teachers are "building up the body of Christ, until we all attain to the unity of the faith and the knowledge of the Son of God, to mature manhood, to the measure of the stature of the fullness of Christ, *so that we may no longer be children*, tossed to and fro by the waves and carried about by every wind of doctrine, by human cunning, by craftiness in deceitful schemes" (Eph 4:12–14, italics added). Stop being "carried away with the error of lawless people and lose your own stability," Peter similarly warns. "But grow in the grace and knowledge of our Lord and Savior Jesus Christ" (2 Pet 3:17–18).

Ours is not the first generation in which young people thought they knew more than their elders. Giving free reign to our desires, ambitions, and tongues is our corruption of the good—that youthful zeal, curiosity, and passion for action that we should carry with us throughout life. As young children, we basically take the world described by our parents and other authority figures for granted. Later, we begin to question things (it's called being a "teenager"). This is as it should be. Adolescence is a great time to explore what we believe and why we believe it, to "own" our faith for ourselves. This assumes, of course, that the grammar has been given to us so that we can actually ask good questions and make informed judgments. A church that stops asking (and allowing) questions betrays its own tenuous grasp of God's truth.

So there are terrific characteristics of young adulthood that should have an important place in the life of the church. At the same time, as I point out in other chapters, we turn virtues into vices. Suspicion of authority, overconfidence, restless and rootless drifting, and anxiety over making commitments have always been weaknesses that we need the whole body to help us grow out of.

Paul tells the church of Corinth that one of the marks of a child is a certain level of restlessness that leads to a lack of depth — a shallow and self-centered spirituality. At Corinth, instead of building each other up, gifted personalities took the stage, asserting themselves above others. It was more like *American Idol* than the body of Christ:

> But I, brothers, could not address you as spiritual people, but as people of the flesh, as infants in Christ. I fed you with milk, not solid food, for you were not ready for it. And even now you are not ready, for you are still of the flesh. For while there is jealousy and strife among you, are you not of the flesh and behaving only in a human way? For when one says, "I follow Paul," and another, "I follow Apollos," are you not being merely human?
>
> What then is Apollos? What is Paul? Servants through whom you believed, as the Lord assigned to each. (1 Cor 3:1–5)

God's church isn't a stage where we perform our solos. It is God's garden. It is a building that God is constructing in his Son, by his Word and Spirit (1 Cor 3:6–9). Against their chaotic worship, he exhorts, "Brothers, do not be children in your thinking" (1 Cor 14:20).

As we grow up, we begin to assume responsibilities — for ourselves and for others. Finding our lives hidden with God in Christ, we are no longer the center of our universe. We press on toward completion in Christ. "Not that I have already obtained this or am already perfect," Paul recognizes, "but I press on to make it my own, because Christ Jesus has made me his own."

> Brothers, I do not consider that I have made it my own. But one thing I do: forgetting what lies behind and straining forward to what lies ahead, I press on toward the goal for the prize of the upward call of God in Christ Jesus. Let those of us who are mature think this way, and if in anything you think otherwise, God will reveal that also to you. Only let us hold true to what we have attained. (Phil 3:12–16)

What is true here for individuals is true also for churches over time. Press on. Don't rest on the laurels of past grace. By all means, test and examine what you have learned. "Only let us hold true to what we have attained." If we're continually starting over from scratch, we'll remain infants. The saving knowledge of Christ is that goal toward which we strive. "Him we proclaim, warning everyone and teaching everyone with all wisdom, that we may present everyone mature in Christ. For this I toil, struggling with all his energy that he powerfully works within me" (Col 1:28–29).

The writer to the Hebrews also encourages us to grow up, to stop behaving like children. Just as he launches into his mind-blowing instruction on Christ's fulfillment of the Melchizedek priesthood, he interrupts himself:

> About this we have much to say, and it is hard to explain, since you have become dull of hearing. For though by this time you ought to be teachers, you need someone to teach you again the basic principles of the oracles of God. You need milk, not solid food, for everyone who lives on milk in unskilled in the word of righteousness, since he is a child. But solid food is for the mature, for those who have their powers of discernment trained by constant practice to distinguish good from evil. (Heb 5:11–14)

To be young is to be restless. Yet as we mature, we learn God's Word and—importantly, as noted above—"powers of discernment *trained by constant practice*." Growth involves leaving behind this restless spirit, learning disciplines that lead to maturity in the faith. If we fail to mature, apostasy is a real danger (Heb 6:1 – 12).

Even in secular societies across time there has been a consensus that wisdom comes with age and experience. This is not to idolize the elderly. After all, "the fathers" in Scripture is a phrase that frequently refers to the wilderness generation that failed to believe God's promise. By contrast, Paul encourages Timothy, "Let no one despise you for your youth, but set the believers an example in speech, in conduct, in love, in faith, in purity" (1 Tim 4:12). In other words, he is to show by his conduct and speech that he is mature, regardless of his age. He has been well-catechized by his mother and grandmother, the apostle reminds him. More than all of this, Paul reminds him of his public ordination to the office. Timothy's authority comes not from his personal charisma, youthful charm, or self-promotion. Rather, it comes from "the gift you have, which was given to you by prophecy when the council of elders laid their hands on you" (4:14). Therefore, Paul says, "until I come, devote yourself to the public reading of Scripture, to exhortation, to teaching" (4:13).

In his instructions to Titus for life in the church, Paul mentions "self-control" four times within the space of twelve verses (Titus 2:1 – 12). "Likewise, urge the younger men to be self-controlled" (2:6). Inclined to self-indulgence, young men especially need to be accountable to pastors and elders. Tragically, self-control is increasingly relinquished among older adults in our shock-jock society. The social pressure imposed by elders to curb enthusiastic outbursts and to reflect before expressing themselves once had considerable cache. The church can become again one place at least where this maturity is encouraged by good examples.

Titus is not a private person asserting his leadership, but holds a public office in the church. Therefore, he is not to be bullied into passivity: "Declare these things; exhort and rebuke with all authority. Let no one disregard you" (Titus 2:15). After all, he is exercising his office, as Christ's representative, not fulfilling his personal agenda. While warning against "shameful gain" and "domineering over those in your charge," Peter nevertheless exhorts elders to assume their vital role. "Likewise, you who are younger, be subject to the elders. Clothe yourselves, all of you, with humility toward one another, for 'God opposes the proud but gives grace to the humble'" (1 Pet 5:2–5).

God's Generations and Ours

It is staggering to contemplate that the transcendent, majestic, sovereign Creator of the cosmos so identifies with a certain people, with a particular history, that he can actually identify himself as "the God *of Israel*," "the God *of the covenant*." "I will be a God to you and to your children after you," he promises; "to a thousand generations," we hear repeatedly in Scripture. Peter reaffirmed this covenantal outlook in his Pentecost sermon: "For the promise is for you and for your children and for all who are far off, everyone whom the Lord our God calls to himself" (Acts 2:39).

God's call comes to us as individuals, but also as families, and it goes out to those who do not yet belong to God's covenant people. The emphasis of his call is on passing on what has been seen and heard: the mighty acts of God in history. The older and wiser members teach and guide the younger.

Israel's calendar of feasts marked these mighty acts and brought the young up to speed on what God has accomplished. Take Passover, for example. "And when your children say to you, 'What do you mean by this service?' you shall say, 'It is the sacrifice of the LORD's Passover, for he passed over the houses of the people of Israel in Egypt, when he struck the Egyptians but spared our houses" (Ex 12:26–27). Christianity is an inherently intergenerational faith because God is faithful from generation to generation, keeping his covenant in spite of his people's unfaithfulness. Instead of inventing beliefs and rites that were judged more relevant to a specific generation, they brought that generation into the atmosphere of the covenant.

God's covenant of grace now unites not only the generations but people "from every tribe and language and people and nation" around the throne of the Lamb (Rev 5:9). It does not follow the consumer cues of this passing age, dividing people according to generations, ethnicity, gender, class, or political parties. In Christ, these walls are broken down. He is now our real location, the marker of our ultimate identity (Gal 3:28).

United to one body with one Head, it is our *differences* from each other that give each part of the body what it needs. The younger need the older. Wealthier believers need the gifts of poorer members. Rather than feed a comfortable narcissism, we need to be enriched by the insights, fellowship, and correction of brothers and sisters from ethnic, political, and economic backgrounds different from our own. The church isn't a circle of friends, but the family of God. The covenant of grace connects generations, rooting them in that worshiping community with the "cloud of witnesses" in heaven as well as here and now (Heb 12:1).

Yet today the market has become the new Pharaoh who defies God's order to let his people go so that they may worship him in the desert at his mountain. "Divide and conquer" is the logic of this new lord. By separating the generations into niche markets, the powers and principalities of this present evil age pick at the covenantal fabric of God's new society. Satan works tirelessly to create gaps between generations in the church — gaps that the fathers and mothers cannot reach across to pass the baton. Someone wisely said, "The church is always one generation from apostasy."

Continuity is the covenantal approach to generations; *novelty* is the decree of our age. Each generation is bombarded with advertisements, ideals, dreams, and expectations that appeal to our collective narcissism. We are special, unique, destined for greatness. Ours is the *truly* revolutionary generation. For those of us reared on "This is not your father's Oldsmobile," it's going to be difficult to sing the Song of Moses: "The LORD is my strength and my song, and he has become my salvation; this is *my* God, and I will praise him, *my father's* God, and I will exalt him" (Ex 15:2, italics added).

In what he calls "a short but self-important history of the Baby Boomer Generation," Joe Queenan, writer for the *New York Times* and *GQ*, makes sport of his generation's "absolute inability to accept the ordinary."[19]

> Because Baby Boomers are obsessed with living in the moment, they insist that every experience be a watershed, every meal extraordinary, every friendship epochal, every concert superb, every sunset meta-celestial. Life isn't like that.... Sunsets are sunsets. By turning spectacularly humdrum occurrences into formal rites, Baby Boomers have transmuted even the most banal activities into "events" requiring reflection, planning, research, underwriting and staggering masses of data. This has essentially ruined everything for everybody else because nothing can ever again be exactly what it was in the first place: something whose very charm is a direct result of its being accessible, near at hand, *ordinary*.[20]

Today we feel the pressure to have our weddings look like the cover of a bridal magazine or movie set. Our marriages have to be made in heaven, even though we're very much on earth. Our presentations at work have to dazzle. Our kids have to make the dean's list and get into the best graduate school. Academic research can't just contribute to knowledge in a field; nothing short of "brilliant" and "groundbreaking" will satisfy if you want a good job. When we do stop and smell the roses, it has to be an unforgettable package at an amazing resort. It's not enough to enjoy recreation at the public park, but *extreme* sports are what really interest us.

By the way, I am not moralizing about these things to be critical of others. In fact, I find myself drawn to these same adrenaline rushes and enticing getaways. My point is that we, as modern Christians, living under the alluring lights of a Las Vegas culture, find it difficult to enjoy more familiar, routine, and common pleasures. Part of the problem is that we want to prove something to ourselves and to others. Even in our down time, we are anxious to set ourselves apart from the rest.

Consider how participation in sports has changed in recent years. Professional sports has become big business, part of the entertainment industry. And now it seems like every year its values trickle down to younger and younger segments of the population. Organized (but not professional) sports used to build character. That was their point. What's new today is not greater drive and measures of excellence, but different goals that require different means and form different patterns. Where playing *for the team* was the point, now it's just an occasion for us (or our children) to stand out. Extracurricular activities have increasingly become a staging area for virtuoso performers who attract the crowds and fetch staggering salaries. A game can no longer just be a game; it has to be a spectacle. And, tragically, the same can be said of many churches.

The Hedonist Paradox

Behind selfish ambition and this exuberant cult of the immediate-experience-in-the-moment lurks a haunting nihilism. We came from nowhere and are going to nowhere, but somewhere in the middle of it all we have to make a big splash. Every moment must be charged with excitement. "If the dead are not raised," Paul famously concluded by quoting a line from a Greek comedy, " 'Let us eat and drink, for tomorrow we die' " (1 Cor 15:32). The technical term for this is *narcissism*.

Even if we pray like Augustine, we often live like the atheistic philosopher Friedrich Nietzsche. His catechism reads:

What is good? Everything that heightens the feeling of power in man, the will to power, power itself.

What is bad? Everything that is born of weakness.

What is happiness? The feeling that power increases—that a resistance is overcome.[21]

In other words, winning *is* everything today. The point isn't even *what* we win, but *that* we win. The goal slips from view—or rather, shifts from someone or something else to ourselves. The problem is that nobody can make us *that* happy, or even as happy as we think we deserve.

Moralists decry our age as *hedonist*. But is that giving ourselves too much credit? At least hedonism has the merit of loving life. The hedonist does not love the God who gives life or acknowledge any accountability to his revealed will; yet he or she at least may fancy the gifts without acknowledging the Giver. Augustine would call this "inordinate desires": longings for that which is good, but by being ranked above God they become idolatrous. For all of their faults, hedonists love life — at least life as they know it apart from God.

Generally speaking, our age displays the opposite tendency. Ironically, in some ways it's more akin to Stoicism. We may know Stoicism as a "stiff upper-lip" approach to life. It evokes the image of the sage sitting in Buddha-like contemplation, immune to the constant flux — and pleasures — of the external world. Stoics emphasized duty and discipline, over against hedonistic drives. However, at the heart of Stoicism is the notion of autonomy: perfect bliss in one's own completeness. The ideal Stoic master has transcended dependence on others. No external need compels, no external threat disturbs the tranquility of his or her self-enclosed existence.

Now, consider iconic characters like James Bond. They find their happiness entirely in themselves. Their serial promiscuity seems to be driven not by need, not even by desire, but merely by arbitrary whim or a transaction calculated to serve their professional aims. One of the delightful features of characters like Jason Bourne is that their tough exterior melts and their dependence on others for their happiness reveals itself. Unlike some of his other characters, Tom Cruise in *Jerry McGuire* is able to tell his girlfriend, "You complete me." He is able to enter into a new phase of the relationship precisely because he is willing to acknowledge his vulnerability: his need to be loved as well as to love. The barrier comes down and invites the other in — all the way into the soul.

But the Stoic tramp is not a lover. There isn't even a sense of adolescent passion, falling in and out of love too easily. Unlike the old-fashioned hedonist, this person's problem is not that he loves too much, but that he doesn't love — or hasn't tried not to love — at all. Friedrich Nietzsche — "the man of azure isolation," as Karl Barth called him — is the sort of person I have in mind here, and it is his attitude that characterizes late modernity. This sort of person works overtime to create an impermeable barrier between self and other.

If you allow yourself to become dependent on others for your happiness, you'll never be happy, because eventually everyone will let you down. So resolve to find your completeness in yourself. Don't let others in.

When you combine this Stoic resolve with arbitrary sexual impulses, the last thing you get is love of life—much less love of another person. Sex takes place purely on the other side of the barrier, in a realm of mutual release—purely physical and external—that can neither threaten nor summon us out of our cocoon to discover, delight in, and desire the other. "No strings attached." There is no covenant—a free exchange of persons and gifts. One may give his or her body to the act, but never the heart and soul. It's just a contract between "consenting adults."

Christianity is far from Stoicism. It affirms desire far more than what we improperly call hedonism. As C. S. Lewis observed, "Our Lord finds our desires, not too strong, but too weak." "We are half-hearted creatures," he adds, "fooling about with drink and sex and ambition when infinite joy is offered us, like an ignorant child who wants to go on making mud pies in a slum because he cannot imagine what is meant by the offer of a holiday at the sea. We are far too easily pleased."[22]

No, to be sure, "hedonism" is too noble a word for this. It's not even a love of life, a lust for something that is in itself a good gift of God. It is no more erotic than the mating of cats outside my window in October and lacks the charm and sociability of diverse mating rituals in the animal kingdom.

There is a problem with our pursuit of the next great experience, our attempts to feed our insatiable appetite for significance. Like excellence and action, happiness needs a worthy object. The pursuit of happiness as an end in itself is "vanity," as we learn from the book of Ecclesiastes. Philosophers call it the "hedonist paradox": the irony that the pursuit of pleasure actually chases it away. "Happiness is like a cat," writes William Bennett. "If you try to coax it or call it, it will avoid you; it will never come. But if you pay no attention to it and go about your business, you'll find it rubbing against your legs and jumping into your lap."[23] Happiness is something that happens when you're looking for someone or something other than happiness. You can't find meaning, fulfillment, or purpose by looking for it, but only by discovering something else. And that discovery comes with careful discernment, which takes time, intentionality, and community.

The same is true of success or impact. Many young people today are filled with anxiety about choosing a major in college. Then they obsess over whether to take a job that has nothing to do with it. They say, "I want to make something of myself, to leave my mark"—or, more altruistically, "to make a difference" in the world. But when we make these desires themselves the object of our life-quest, they become idols. Like all idols, they overpromise and underdeliver. When they fail us, we become bitterly unhappy. Since we can't really get much reaction from an idol, we begin to resent other people who were their messengers.

We do not find success by trying to be successful or happiness by trying to be happy. Rather, we find these things by attending to the skills, habits, and—to be honest—the often *dull* routines that make us even modestly successful at anything. If you are always looking for an impact, a legacy, and success, you will not take the time to care for the things that matter.

We Want It All: Autonomy and Community

A spate of books in recent years points up the narcissistic tendency that makes genuine growth and community difficult in virtually every area of life. Over a decade ago, David Brooks identified the Boomer generation as "Bobos in Paradise."[24] On one hand, they demand autonomy, resisting settled beliefs, norms, and values. They want to do it and have it their way. On the other hand, they crave community and belonging. You cannot have it both ways, though. Belonging to a community requires individuals to live within a certain level of mutual accountability.

But misery loves company and I take some perverse comfort in learning that this anxious narcissism isn't just a Boomer phenomenon.

Led by Jean Twenge, a group of psychologists followed trends among the Busters, also known as Generation X (1965–83) and especially the Millennials or Generation Y (since 1984). The title of Twenge's book reporting the findings is telling: *Generation Me: Why Today's Young Americans Are More Confident, Assertive, Entitled—And More Miserable Than Ever Before.*[25]

Judging by recent studies, the Boomers' children and grand-children are if anything even *more* intense in their struggle with this inner contradiction between autonomy and community. Wanting to belong, to be part of something larger than themselves, they soon realize that communities are inherently limiting. There is no community without consensus: a basic, shared agreement about the things that define it. You have to show up in order to belong. And shared agreements have to be patrolled (disciplined) in order to be maintained and to endure through the various crises that individual members might provoke.

So people get anxious about making commitments. "You are better off leaving your options open," they are told. And, wow, what options there are! We can scour the Web for bits and pieces of the identity that we are crafting for ourselves and the accessories that we think will help us pull it off. The choices are endless—and, therefore, both overwhelming and anxiety-producing. People seem to be (or at least are expected to be) in the middle of making a new life-altering choice at every moment.

For Boomers, this wonderland of consumerism is fascinating—still a bit novel. Yet for Millennials and those coming along after them, it is normal—so normal that it becomes boring. The world of choices and limitless options is no longer a trip to the carnival; it's their home. The experience of young people today is not one of being uprooted as much as of not having had any roots to begin with. As numerous studies indicate, this is just as true in evangelical churches, where the average person raised in our circles cannot articulate even the basic message of Christianity. (This is in sharp contrast with Mormons and Muslims, for example.)

The Internet is the quarry from which younger generations craft their own selves and then advertise a desired persona on Facebook. A new word has been invented to describe the source of information and identity: wiki, the Hawaiian word for quick. Due in part to economic instability, Millennials are more cautious — even a little anxious — about the future. Marrying later, and having children even later still, the idea of being "tied down" is even more disconcerting.

Deep Sea Diving in a Jet-Ski Age

Psychiatrist Keith Ablow joins the chorus of his colleagues along with sociologists and historians in a recent online article, where he argues a simple premise: "We are raising a generation of deluded narcissists."[26] Today's college students "are more likely than ever to call themselves gifted and driven to succeed, even though their test scores and time spent studying are decreasing." A number of recent studies point up "the toxic psychological impact of media and technology on children, adolescents and young adults, particularly as it regards turning them into faux celebrities — the equivalent of lead actors in their own fictionalized life stories." He adds:

> On Facebook, young people can fool themselves into thinking they have hundreds or thousands of "friends." They can delete unflattering comments. They can block anyone who disagrees with them or pokes holes in their inflated self-esteem. They can choose to show the world only flattering, sexy or funny photographs of themselves (dozens of albums full, by the way), "speak" in pithy short posts and publicly connect to movie stars and professional athletes and musicians they "like." Using Twitter, young people can pretend they are worth "following," as though they have real-life fans, when all that is really happening is the mutual fanning of false love and false fame. Using computer games, our sons and daughters can pretend they are Olympians, Formula 1 drivers, rock stars or sharpshooters.... On MTV and other networks, young people can see lives just like theirs portrayed on reality TV shows fueled by such incredible self-involvement and self-love that any of the "real-life" characters should really be in psychotherapy to have any chance at anything like a normal life. These are the psychological drugs of

the 21st Century and they are getting our sons and daughters very sick, indeed.

Tragically, narcissism frequently leads to self-loathing. As Ablow says, "False pride can never be sustained." Young people are looking for more highs to define and distinguish themselves. "They're doing anything to distract themselves from the fact that they feel empty inside and unworthy." However, the bubble will burst. Ablow warns, "Watch for an epidemic of depression and suicidality, not to mention homicidality, as the real self-loathing and hatred of others that lies beneath all this narcissism rises to the surface."

Technology has always rearranged our social and psychic furniture. As Jesuit priest and media scholar John Culkin pointed out, "We shape our tools and thereafter they shape us."[27] Ever since the printing press, evangelicals have always been at the front of the line for new technologies for spreading the Word. Radio, TV, the Web, and worship with rock bands, video clips, and PowerPoint presentations have become common.

There are two easy responses to technological innovation: embrace it or reject it. As evangelicals, we have a tendency to embrace popular culture, with its bent toward the ephemeral. Ironically, while we jazz up our worship spaces with gadgets and glitz, it is often specialists of technology and culture who caution greater reflection. One thinks of Marshal McLuhan's *The Medium Is the Message* and Neil Postman's *Amusing Ourselves to Death*. In his bestseller, *The Shallows*, Nicholas Carr argues that in the Internet age we are losing our capacity for deep thinking, reading, and conversation. Instead of deep sea divers, he says, we jet ski on a sea of words and especially images.[28] Having taught a generation of students to develop new technologies, MIT professor Sherry Turkle raises this question from a commonsense perspective. The title of one of her recent books tells the story: *Alone Together: Why We Expect More of Technology and Less of Each Other.*[29] Despite their fondness for theological novelty, liberal Protestantism is typically more indebted to high culture with its conservative suspicion of technology.

Part of growing up is developing discernment. Even where

Scripture does not give us explicit direction, we have to continually ask each other how the tools we use help or hinder the growth of God's garden (growth in depth as well as breadth). New technologies can't be all bad, but then they can't be all good either. That's where wisdom comes in. Wisdom discerns not just between good and bad but between better and best. However, before they can even develop critical skills, younger generations are submerged in a sea of data, images, and ads.

Most of us have to stretch our historical imagination to understand a world that was normal not that long ago. With our automobile-driven culture of climate-controlled suburbia, anonymous individualism deposits us in our garage without having to bother with others. Add to that now the isolation of having the world at your fingertips in front of a screen — TV, Internet, and phone — and it's easy to see why we've become quite different people in barely a generation. In a recent story on NPR, an older woman was talking about how train passengers used to bring baskets of food on the trip from Madrid to Paris, exchanging cheese, meats, and fruit among themselves. Now, she said, there are no baskets; they all sit alone, glued to their gadgets.

The spoken word, as a medium, is socializing. It puts you in the middle of an event instead of in front of a screen. According to Scripture, God *spoke* the world into being by his powerful word (Ps 33:6). The eternal Son is the *Word* of God. Jesus himself said, "The words that I have spoken to you are spirit and life" (John 6:63). The apostles taught that "faith comes from hearing, and hearing through the word of Christ" (Rom 10:17) and that we are born again through the preaching of the gospel (Rom 1:16; Eph 1:13 – 14; 1 Thess 1:5; 1 Pet 1:23; Jas 1:18). But we are turned in on ourselves as fallen creatures, and our growing captivity to texting and tweeting only deepens the tendency. We do not hear God address us in church, nor do we "store up [God's] word in [our] heart" (Ps 119:11) since we can access the data on our smartphones.

On one hand, we are addicted to distractions (euphemistically called "multi-tasking"). On the other hand, like salty peanuts, all of this clicking, cutting-and-pasting, Googling and chatting, posting and texting just creates a deeper thirst for something more meaningful. Younger generations will say that they long for community, but the habits that they've acquired—and which are now deeply woven into the fabric of their personality—make it difficult for them to belong to any particular group with any serious and long-term investment. Breaking away from the herd to "be yourself" may have been an exhilarating rebellion in the days of "Leave It To Beaver." But when *everybody's* doing his own thing, there's no fun left in being a rebel.

There are plenty of terrific ways in which social media connect us, but calling any of these *communities* seems like a bit of hyperbole. Community requires coherence, cohesion, and consensus—over time and, depending on the type of community, across spatial borders as well. Unlike Internet connections, deep community requires face-to-face, embodied engagement and accountability. You can't just "unfriend" your next-door neighbor, much less your spouse or children, without daily repercussions. It also requires an agreement to live within that consensus. This is true for contractual relationships like those we have with service providers and banks, but all the more for covenantal institutions like marriage, family, and church.

In addition to the problem of constantly looking for significance, anxiously hoping that our lives will have a lasting impact, is our addiction to instantaneous results. If anything, younger generations are even more habituated to immediate gratification than their parents and grandparents. This is due less to their conscious choices than to social practices that have made them what they are—practices that reshape all of us in profound ways. For example, many of those in younger generations do not recall having sent or received a handwritten letter. Instead of composing a letter by hand, perhaps rethinking something we said and coming back to correct it, we blurt out scores of trivial messages. Sure, much has been gained with email and texting—especially the ease with which we can be in touch with many people. Still, much is lost, such as intimacy, reflective interaction and relationships, and care. The medium makes a difference.

Everything today must be quick and easy, because that is how the world seems to operate now. We falsely assume that we must change or we'll be left behind. In the past couple of decades we've heard that churches still committed to the public ministry of preaching, sacraments, and worship will be like pay phones—that we need to "reboot" Christianity. One writer even suggests that the churches of tomorrow will be more like Wikipedia: de-institutionalized, quick, and democratic.

The point is that the movements that wash over us are largely determined by the attachment of evangelicalism to pop culture, which inevitably means youth culture. It may be exciting for the moment, but it is not sustainable and it does not serve well an inter-generational covenant of grace. Reaching non-Christians with "the faith ... once for all delivered to the saints" (Jude 1:3) requires zeal *and* knowledge. Keeping the generations connected requires love and patience on all sides. The elders must be attentive to any disconnection expressed by the younger believers, and younger generations need to be less enamored of their own relevance as they assume their important place in the body of Christ.

The key to maturity is *time* and *community*. Discernment takes time and a lot of godly input spanning generations and ethnicities. There's a reason why the Psalms have been sung for thousands of years, and why many young people still know "Amazing Grace," even if they barely know "Shine, Jesus, Shine" and have never (happily) even heard of "In the Garden." A consensus of believers in churches over a few generations has a way of weeding out the less edifying songs.

If staying with the familiar (no matter how bad it may be) is the tendency of a conservative temperament, the ideal of creativity and novelty—as an end in itself—becomes destructive of long conversations. At the end of a term, a student discovered the professor's evaluation explaining the poor grade: "Your paper is original and creative. The parts that are creative are not original and the parts that are original are not very good." The best changes are slow, incremental, and deliberate. Instead of cutting their own path, they extend the ancient faith into the next generation.

Wisdom challenges our youthful restlessness without quenching its zeal. It does not reduce the faith to a few important doctrines or offer a menu of options for creating one's own. Remember, the past and the present are basically the same in at least one important respect. Both occupy the period identified in Scripture as "this present age" that is "passing away." It is the powers of "the age to come" that are breaking in on us now, as they did on our forebears. If this is true, then neither the past nor the present is normative. It is the canon of Scripture that renders both relative and open to correction.

The key is to be able to distinguish between goals that can be achieved quickly and those that require more time and care, and to be able to value the latter as something worth waiting for. It is not difficult to compare a list of things that are quick and easy, yielding immediate results, with a list of goods that require long-term investment, care, growing expertise, and maturity. Aren't most of the things we value most on that second sheet? And is it any wonder that we're miserable if we do not care about things that take time, require submission to a community, and do not yield immediate and measurable results?

So it is time for all of us to grow up. It's time for gifted communicators and leaders to become pastors, for restless souls to submit to the encouragement and correction in the body, for movements to give way to churches. As many are learning in emerging nations, especially in the aftermath of the Arab Spring, the energy of the masses gathered in the square can be exhilarating; the hard part is forming a working, living, growing set of institutions that can sustain a state over the long haul. Movements typically don't like institutions. They live off the memory of the extraordinary moment and find it difficult to move in a united way toward a sustainable environment for generations. But the church, despite current appearances, is God's emerging ecosystem of the new creation.

Instead of allowing youthful passion for the new and revolutionary to dominate our families and churches, let's begin to recover our role as adults who discover and then hand over hidden treasures that we've been stumbling over each day in our own flight from the ordinary.

Exercise

1. Divide a sheet of paper. On the left side write down the things that are quick and easy, yielding immediate results. On the right side, list the things that require long-term investment, care, growing expertise, and maturity. Evaluate the relative value of each side of the sheet.

2. What are some of the characteristics of youth (positive and negative), and how does Scripture encourage maturity? Does Christianity in our culture today seem too youth-driven?

3. What is the "Hedonist's Paradox"? And do you feel the inner contradiction between autonomy (having things your way) and community (submitting to others)?

4. How does the technology we use shape us, for better and worse? Divide two columns under the headings, "Appropriate" and "Inappropriate," and consider what uses of technology may be right for one context but not for another.

CHAPTER 4

the next big thing

Seotember 2003 marked a turning point in the development of Western civilization." So begins an intriguing study by Joseph Heath and Andrew Potter.[30]

That was the month that *Adbusters* magazine started accepting orders for the Black Spot Sneaker, its own signature brand of "subversive" running shoes. After that day, no rational person could possibly believe that there is a tension between "mainstream" and "alternative" culture. After that day, it became obvious to everyone that cultural rebellion, of the type epitomized by *Adbusters* magazine, was not a threat to the system — it *is* the system.

Subversive running shoes! Seriously? The radical is now ordinary and "countercultural" now simply defines culture. Alternative rock quickly became mainstream. Even the garage band that pioneers a new sound is soon a commodity owned and marketed. To leave your mark, you have to distinguish your brand in the marketplace. But, of course, that means that pop culture simply is opposed to culture — that is, not only to current offerings, but to anything and everything that has gone before it. You can't just build ingeniously on the wisdom of the past, you have to reinvent. Even sneakers have to be "subversive."

Enamored of its reported amazingness, each generation razes the empire to its foundations and starts over until the next generation has its own go at it. This means, of course, that everyone born of a woman must feel deep inside the primal duty to shake things up.

The problem is that there is little left to rebel against—and certainly little that has been around long enough to represent a tradition to overthrow. No longer stone fortresses, our "Bastilles" become Styrofoam sets on a Disney stage. The reforming of something substantial has enduring influence. But perpetual reinvention dooms cultures—and churches—to passing shadows of momentary glamour with few lasting legacies beyond the trivial. How can I say that with so much confidence? Because the engineers and marketers of each new movement themselves report with thorough analysis the demise of the one that just preceded theirs.

Perpetual shock is the new normal in the church as well. It seems like Jesus needs rebranding every couple of decades. Commonly, the rhetoric of radical in our churches actually mirrors our culture, even when—no, *especially* when—it invokes the lingo of "countercultural," "subversive," "alternative," "extreme," and so forth. The likes of Athanasius, Augustine, Bernard, Luther, and Calvin sought to *reform* the church. But for centuries now radical Protestants have been trying to reboot, reinvent, start over, and reconstitute the *real* church of the true saints over against the ordinary churches. For that level of enthusiasm, of course, you have to be in a state of perpetual innovation, like Apple and Black Spot Sneaker.

Each new wave of revival rushes in like a tsunami and carries much of the settled coastline out to sea. While in past ages faithfulness was measured by continuity, every new movement has to prove itself in the market by the extent to which it breaks away from everything that has gone before it. To parody the last line in the observation above about the *Adbusters* magazine, ecclesiastical rebellion is not a threat to the system—it *is* the system. In fact, historians give us a lot of reasons to believe that evangelical Protestantism today is being shaped by the cult of perpetual novelty.

Every now and again, of course, things do need to be shaken up. But in our culture it's hard to know when one earthquake ends and another begins—especially with all of the aftershocks in between. Because the Word of God is "living and active," always breaking into this present age of sin and death with its penetrating energies of judgment and grace, the church is always subject to correction. That's what keeps the church from curving in on itself, like any other long-running corporation. Yet this Word doesn't just tear down, it builds up; and building up takes a long time and care, across many generations. Weeds have to be pulled. Limbs have to be trimmed. Sometimes a tree here or there has to be chopped down before its disease spreads to the other plants. But you don't bulldoze the garden and start over again.

In his *Screwtape Letters*, C. S. Lewis has the veteran demon tell his apprentice that "the horror of the same old thing" is "one of the most valuable passions we have produced in the human heart." The discussion follows about how *fashion, novelty*, and *change* will certainly produce an insatiable desire for, ironically, more of the same. "This demand is valuable in various ways. In the first place it diminishes pleasure while increasing desire. The pleasure of novelty is by its very nature more subject than any other to the law of diminishing returns."[31] Here's more from Screwtape on the matter:

> The game is to have them running about with fire extinguishers whenever there is a flood, and all crowding to that side of the boat which is already nearly gunwale under. Thus we make it fashionable to expose the dangers of enthusiasm at the very moment when they are all really becoming worldly and lukewarm; a century later, when we are really making them all Byronic and drunk with emotion, the fashionable outcry is directed against the dangers of the mere "understanding."[32]

The present chapter follows naturally from the previous one. After all, the cult of The Next Big Thing is always the assertion of a new generation of emerging adults. Movements are largely youth-driven, whereas institutions are usually run by elders. The challenge, especially in the church where we are drawn together in Christ from different ethnicities, socioeconomic backgrounds, and generations, is to be "eager to maintain the unity of the Spirit in the bond of peace" (Eph 4:3).

Our culture celebrates The Next Big Thing, but Scripture speaks of an intergenerational covenant of grace. You can't keep taking your line out of the water, repotting the plant, constantly taking the temperature, or redirecting your entire focus and strategy every minute. You have to let the King run his kingdom, follow his instructions, and become a disciple as well as make them. "A watched pot never boils," the experienced chef tells her impatient apprentice.

I am not suggesting that traditionalism is a good alternative. Through the Word, the Holy Spirit breaks up the harmonies of this present age. And yet, whenever he tears down, he also builds up. And building up takes time. As G. K. Chesterton observed in 1924:

> The whole modern world has divided itself into Conservatives and Progressives. The business of Progressives is to go on making mistakes. The business of Conservatives is to prevent mistakes from being corrected. Even when the revolutionist might himself repent of his revolution, the traditionalist is already defending it as part of his tradition. Thus we have two great types — the advanced person who rushes us into ruin, and the retrospective person who admires the ruins. He admires them especially by moonlight, not to say moonshine.[33]

The answer to progressivism and traditionalism is the same: being open to the never-changing and yet always-new power of God's Word as our only norm for faith and practice. So let's allow the parade to pass us by as it marches behind The Next Big Thing. Instead, let's do a little spring cleaning each day. There will be some forgotten treasures amid a lot of clutter. "But examine everything carefully; hold fast to that which is good" (1 Thess 5:21 NASB).

The Next Big Thing *Is* a Tradition

Growing up in evangelical churches, I didn't think I was shaped by a tradition. In fact, "tradition" was not ordinarily a positive term. We were Bible-believing Christians. We just said and did what the Bible taught. It was others — especially "high church" folks — who followed a tradition. We, however, were just plain Christians.

In reality, though, I was reared in a tradition. It was in many ways a rich and edifying tradition. To be specific, it was evangelical

Protestantism of a specific stripe. Often without knowing it, this tradition preserved many elements of orthodox Christianity that many so-called traditional churches were throwing overboard.

Although these churches did not subscribe to creeds and confessions, they were in many ways more committed to orthodox doctrines than many churches that recited them each week. This tradition mediated to me, mostly informally, a basic familiarity with the Bible and a living knowledge of the gospel of salvation by grace, through faith in Christ. Yet this tradition was also the product of the Radical Reformation, pietism, and American revivalism. So the emphases of the Reformers, such as Luther and Calvin, sat uncomfortably alongside the more Arminian — even Semi-Pelagian and outright Pelagian — emphases of Charles Finney and Benjamin Franklin. It was the tradition of a distinctly American revivalism with its curious mixture of separatism and civil religion.

Simply identifying the historical sources and trajectories of Christian communities doesn't stop the conversation ("You have your tradition and I have mine"). On the contrary, it allows us to acknowledge our own tradition, to analyze it in its particulars for faithfulness to Scripture, and to engage other traditions with respect. Dutch theologian and statesman Abraham Kuyper noted in 1898:

> There is, to be sure, a theological illusion abroad ... which conveys the impression that, with the Holy Scriptures in hand, one can independently construct theology.... This illusion is a denial of the historic and organic character of theology, and for this reason is inwardly untrue. No theologian following the direction of his own compass would ever have found by himself what he now confesses and defends on the ground of Holy Scripture. By far the largest part of his results is adopted by him from theological tradition, and even the proofs he cites from Scripture, at least as a rule, have not been discovered by himself, but have been suggested to him by his predecessors.[34]

One of the prominent Christian "traditions" today is nondenominational evangelicalism. To deny that this is a tradition is to cut off the possibility of internal evaluation, critique, and reform.

Ironically, it tends to create the most resistant sort of traditionalism. Bereft of criticism by God's Word from the past or by representatives of other traditions in the present, allegedly nondenominational and nontraditional churches become bound to their own circle of living Bible teachers, movements, and emphases that have their own unacknowledged history.

For example, the churches of my youth would have said that the church down the street was following tradition rather than Scripture. Yet when I began asking why we didn't baptize infants, it was hard to find a good explanation beyond "we believe the Bible." Even at a young age, it caused me to wonder whether that was just another way of saying "we follow our tradition."

To be clear, I am not saying that there aren't those who defend their views on topics like this from Scripture, much less that Scripture itself doesn't give us clear answers. Nor am I saying that tradition determines truth. Yet it is important to recognize that we never come to the Bible as the first Christians, but always as those who have been inducted into a certain set of expectations about what we will find in Scripture. I did not find the doctrine of the Trinity all by myself. It is part of the rich inheritance in the communion of saints from the past and the present. So the best way forward is to respect and evaluate our traditions, not to idolize or ignore them.

The current impulse toward radical Christianity, then, is itself part of a tradition that is rooted in successive waves of radical Protestantism. The magisterial Reformers like Luther and Calvin sought to reform the church, not to start over. Unlike the radicals, they believed the church had continued from the time of the apostles. It was the medieval church that had introduced novelties in doctrine and worship, they argued, and they sought to recover the best of the ancient church. American Christianity—even in denominations that identify as Lutheran and Reformed—have been closer in many ways to the radical sects than to the evangelical Reformers.

The Reformers recognized the supremacy of God's Word over the church's doctrine and practice. Yet they also realized that the Spirit illumines the church to understand the inspired text. The history of the church is the story of both the Spirit's illumination and the ongoing sinfulness of human beings, including believers, to read and follow it properly. Although it is subservient to Scripture, tradition was taken seriously as a guide to interpretation. Creeds and confessions reflected a common understanding of the Bible's basic teachings. All believers must have equal access to Christ and his Word, but there was no "right of private interpretation." Rather, we all read the Bible together, submitting to the common mind of the church through its representative bodies.

The Reformers also believed that every believer was a priest, able to go directly to God and to intercede for each other. But they held as firmly that the New Testament appoints pastors to preach, baptize, and administer Communion and elders to supervise the church's spiritual health.

The Reformers believed that God alone saves. Salvation is not an asset or treasury owned by the hierarchy, to be administered to those who follow the prescribed rules. It is God's free favor and gift. Nevertheless, they taught just as clearly that God works ordinarily through the ministry of human beings as they preach, baptize, administer the Lord's Supper, and guide the doctrine and life of believers in Christ's name.

On each of these points, the radicals went further. The visible church is false; the invisible church of the truly born-again and Spirit-filled must reinvent the church of Acts. The priesthood of all believers meant that every true believer was a minister and could preach, baptize, or serve Communion. And the Spirit works directly and immediately, often through extraordinary revelations. It is not the "outer" Word and sacraments that matter, but the "inner" voice of the Spirit and an inner washing and presence of Jesus apart from water, bread, and wine. Everything that is external, institutional, visible, physical, formal, and official is opposed to that which is internal, individual, invisible, immaterial, and informal. Genuine faith is spontaneous, not mediated through structured ministry. According to Separatist leader John Smyth, those who are "born again ...

should no longer need means of grace," since the persons of the God-head "are better than all scriptures, or creatures whatsoever."[35]

Though evangelicals today might differ on the details (such as not needing Scripture), John Smyth seems to have won out. No longer reform, but revolution. No longer repairing the ramparts that have fallen, but demolition and reconstruction. No longer ordinary growth—both of believers during their lifetime and churches generally through history—but extraordinary movements would lead us into the age of the Spirit. Authority shifted from the external Word, communally heard, embraced, and lived, to the individual's experience. All of this raises the question as to the extent to which evangelicalism has, for some time, been as much the facilitator as the victim of modern autonomy.

Every new movement comes with fresh press releases about restoring the fallen church (rather than reforming the partly faithful/partly unfaithful church), a rebirth of the church of Acts, a new Pentecost, and even a rebooting that will change everything. Yet, at the end of the day, they all reflect a fairly unbroken tradition from the radical sects of centuries past. Each movement began as a democratic leveling, eradicating structures, special offices, liturgies, sometimes even preaching and sacraments. And yet, nondenominational movements soon became ... denominations. Radical innovations soon became unquestioned traditions.

Longing for Revival

A lot of what has distinguished American culture—the cult of celebrity, youthfulness, and innovation—was born on the sawdust trail of the revivalists. The cult of The Next Big Thing—whether a new rock band, a diet fad, a political movement, or a spiritual explosion or religious crusade—is not the result simply of our captivity to culture; the wider cultural phenomenon may never have emerged without revivalism. In a society before TV, revivals were not just influenced by pop culture. They *were* pop culture.

There are two ways to understand revival. The first is to see it as a "surprising work of God," God's "extraordinary blessing on his ordinary means of grace." That is how Jonathan Edwards saw it, as Ian Murray summarizes.[36] God is utterly free to withhold or send revival as he pleases.

The second approach sees revival as something within our control—something that can be staged and managed with predictable results. If you follow the right steps, you'll get the right outcomes. Basically, it's a technological approach to religion. Like a genie in a bottle, even God is subject to the laws of cause and effect. In the words of the nineteenth-century evangelist Charles Finney (a key promoter of this second view), "A revival is not a miracle or dependent on a miracle in any sense. It is simply the philosophical result of the right use of means like any other effect." The radical Protestant impulse for extraordinary evidence, through extraordinary methods, became especially pronounced with Charles Finney. Finney defined his "new measures" as "inducements sufficient to convert sinners with."[37]

Ironically, beneath the veneer of an outpouring of the Spirit, this sort of revivalism was more like deism: God had set up these laws and now it's up to us. I get the same feeling when I encounter prosperity evangelists. For all the talk of miracles, these wonders turn out to be natural after all. Follow the prescribed steps and you get your miracle. Do you even really need God in this sort of scheme, except as the architect who set everything up this way?

Constant pressure was placed on the ingenuity of the evangelist to keep up the emotional temperature. Not only an extraordinary conversion experience at the beginning, but perpetual shaking and quaking are necessary. "A revival will decline and cease," Finney warned, "unless Christians are frequently re-converted."[38] A revival could be planned, staged, and managed. The Great Commission just said, "Go," according to Finney. "*It did not prescribe any forms.* It did not admit any.... And [the disciples'] object was to make known the gospel in the *most effectual way* ... so as to obtain attention and secure obedience of the greatest number possible. No person can find any *form* of doing this laid down in the Bible."[39]

Just as the new birth lies entirely in the hands of the individual, through whatever "excitements" are likely to "induce repentance," the church is conceived primarily as a society of moral reformers. In a letter on revival, Finney issued the following, "Now the great business of the church is to reform the world — to put away every kind of sin. The church of Christ was originally organized to be a body of reformers ... to reform individuals, communities, and governments." If the churches will not follow, they will simply have to be left behind.[40] In other words, they have to think like a movement rather than a church.

John Williamson Nevin, a Reformed contemporary of Finney, contrasted what he called "the system of the bench" (precursor to the altar call) and "the system of the catechism":

> The old Presbyterian faith, into which I was born, was based throughout on the idea of covenant family religion, church membership by God's holy act in baptism, and following this a regular catechetical training of the young, with direct reference to their coming to the Lord's table. In one word, all proceeded on the theory of sacramental, educational religion.[41]

These two systems, Nevin concluded, "involve at the bottom two different theories of religion."

Nevin's conclusion has been justified by subsequent history. Toward the end of his ministry, as he considered the condition of many who had experienced his revivals, Finney himself wondered if this endless craving for ever-greater experiences might lead to spiritual exhaustion.[42] In fact, his worries were justified. The area where Finney's revivals were especially dominant is now referred to by historians as the "burned-over district," a seedbed of both disillusionment and the proliferation of esoteric sects.[43]

Eventually, the ideal of a measurable conversion experience not only augmented but was set over against the real but steady growth for which there could not be a standard formula of measurement. There were steps and obvious signs that you could check off to know if you were really "in." Eventually, the routinization of conversion procedures — like those of the factories in the Industrial

Revolution — could be calculated, measured, and reproduced. This is what happened in Anglo-American revivalism.

Each successive awakening or revival claimed to be radical, dispensing with the baggage of the past that weighs down mission. In relation to the history of the church, these movements are indeed radical. Yet they have been anything but countercultural, especially in the American context. The values of democracy and free enterprise — grounded in individual choice — became the gospel itself in the Second Great Awakening.

The church growth movement was as culturally (and even politically) bound as its critics have argued. And yet, one of the movement's most vocal critics — the Emergent Movement — seems no less tethered to cultural fads. We hear once again the usual "get-with-it-or-get-left-behind" messages. We have to start over, we are told, with ordinary-ministry churches compared to pay phones: they still exist, but nobody uses them. Like most rebellions, it reflects undiscerning reactions to what it identifies, perhaps legitimately, as unthinking consumerism. It is easy simply to switch political parties. It takes little effort to determine one's doctrinal convictions, cultural and moral sympathies, and ecclesial practices by simple antithesis. "Everything Must Change!" Away with pastors preaching sermons; let's make it more of a dialogue with the Bible as one of the conversation partners. We share our journeys. In any case, it's not about going to church but about being the church, not about hearing the gospel but being the gospel. Informed discernment is something that evangelicalism, across all of its "tribes," seems to need desperately right now.

There are many today who think like Edwards but act like Finney. In *Head and Heart*, Catholic historian Garry Wills observes:

> The camp meeting set the pattern for credentialing Evangelical ministers. They were validated by the crowd's response. Organizational credentialing, doctrinal purity, personal education were useless here — in fact, some educated ministers had to make a pretense of ignorance. The minister was ordained from below, by the converts he made. This was an even more democratic procedure

than electoral politics, where a candidate stood for office and spent some time campaigning. This was a spontaneous and instant proclamation that the Spirit accomplished. The do-it-yourself religion called for a make-it-yourself ministry.[44]

Wills repeats Richard Hofstadter's conclusion that "the star system was not born in Hollywood but on the sawdust trail of the revivalists."[45]

There are numerous instructions in the New Testament on church offices and qualifications, preaching, the sacraments, public prayer, and discipline. In striking contrast, there are no instructions on—or even examples of—revival. What we meet in the book of Acts is the account of the Spirit's extraordinary work through the apostles. Throughout Luke's account, we encounter the expression, "And the word of God spread." That's how God's garden was growing. Their ministry, along with the signs and wonders certifying it, remain the indelible marks of the truth of their message for us today. Like Good Friday and Easter, Pentecost was an unrepeatable event in the history of redemption, and it is a gift that keeps on giving, through the ordinary ministry.

Many of the reasons we offer for needing revival (lethargy in evangelism and missions, lack of heartfelt experience of God's grace, coldness in prayer, rising vice and infidelity, social evils, etc.) are problems that the *ordinary* ministry is supposed to address each week. Not only may the longing for revival lead us to treat this ministry as humdrum; it can subtly justify an unacceptable state of affairs in the meantime. Another question is the extent to which a longing for revival has been woven into civil religion. The antidote to a sagging moral nerve and patriotic fervor is a revival. Among other problems, this turns the gospel into a means to an end. No longer is the church's mission to deliver Christ with all of his saving benefits to sinners; it is chiefly to act as the "soul of the nation," to lead it onward and upward toward its exceptional destiny.

This has been the vicious cycle of evangelical revivalism ever since: a pendulum swinging between enthusiasm and disillusionment rather than steady maturity in Christ through participation in the ordinary life of the covenant community. The regular preaching of Christ from all of the Scriptures, baptism, the Supper, the prayers of confession and praise, and all of the other aspects of ordinary Christian fellowship are seen as too ordinary. Whether one agrees with that will depend largely on whether one believes that God saves sinners or we save ourselves with God's help.

Driven to and fro with every wind of doctrine and often no doctrine at all, those reared in evangelicalism become accustomed to hype and cataclysmic events of intense spiritual experience that nevertheless wear off. When they do wear off, there is often little to keep them from trying a different form of spiritual therapy or dropping out of the religion rat race altogether.

It will come as no surprise by now that I prefer the first approach: revival as God's extraordinary blessing on his ordinary means of grace. Looking back through church history, we can see some remarkable moments when — against all human odds — the Spirit blessed the ministry of his Word in extraordinary ways. If the Lord were to send another blessing of that sort, we should delight in his surprising grace.

The earlier revival preachers, most notably Edwards and Whitefield — and to a large extent John Wesley — still believed that revival was an extraordinary blessing on God's ordinary means of grace. In the book of Acts we find many examples of obvious conversion experiences — frequently associated with extraordinary phenomena. Yet it is always through the ministry of the Word. Even when an angel appeared to the Roman centurion Cornelius in Acts 10, the message was to send for Peter to come and preach the gospel to him, his household, and his soldiers. Hearing the message, Cornelius and many others believed and were baptized. So even in the era of the extraordinary ministry of the apostles, the ordinary means of grace are front and center.

However, even when it is seen as a free work of God that we have no right to demand and no power to control, does focusing on revival contribute to our dissatisfaction with God's ordinary blessing on his ordinary means? I'm inclined to think that it does — and has.

We see this danger even in the first Great Awakening. It has been argued that George Whitefield was America's first celebrity. This is not to impugn his character. Whitefield displayed remarkable humility in many ways. Up and down the Atlantic seaboard, though, his revival events divided churches. To question the innovative methods being employed was to quench the Spirit. Denunciations of various pastors as unconverted, simply because they questioned the revival, divided even colonial Calvinists.

So while we have every reason to distinguish revival as Edwards and Whitefield understood it from revivalism as it came to be identified with Finney and the Second Great Awakening, I want to press the deeper question: Is the intense longing for revival itself part of the problem, fueling the feverish expectation for The Next Big Thing? Is it not remarkable enough that Jesus Christ himself is speaking to us whenever his Word is preached each week? Is it not a miracle enough that a lush garden is blooming in the desert of this present evil age? Is it not enough of a wonder that the Spirit is still raising those who are spiritually dead to life through this preached gospel? Is water baptism an outward pledge that we make in response to a decision we made to be born again? Or is it a means of God's miraculous grace? And is it not sufficient that those who belong to Christ are growing in the grace and knowledge of his Word, strengthened in their faith by the regular administration of the Supper, common fellowship in doctrine, prayer, and praise, guided by elders and served by deacons? Doesn't the longing for revival tend to create the impression that between revivals you have lulls where the Spirit is not active at least in the same power or degree of power through these means Christ appointed?

From a New Testament perspective, what happens every day in churches across America and around the world is what really matters in terms of repentance and faith. The problem is that many of the churches longing for revival to fix our spiritual ills as a nation are unwitting carriers of secularization to the people in the pews each week. It is not just this revival or that revival, in my view, but the longing for revival itself that works against the patient, difficult, often tedious, and yet marvelously effective means that God has ordained for expanding his kingdom. Pragmatism becomes the norm. The past and present are to be forgotten. God is doing something completely new among us that cannot be contained in the old jars. It is this way of thinking that dislodges us from faithful preaching, administration of the sacraments, and mutual accountability for life and doctrine in the communion of saints.

Conversion and Covenantal Nurture

If our Christian life is grounded in a radical experience, we will keep looking for repeat performances. Not slow growth in the same direction, but radical spikes in the graph. This keeps us always on the prowl for The Next Big Thing.

Conversion and covenantal nurture go hand-in-hand in Scripture. Evangelism is not something reserved for unbelievers we invite to a special service. It's the weekly mission to the saved and the lost alike. There is no opposition between personal faith in Christ and the ministry of the church, "getting saved" and "joining a church." Peter declared in his Pentecost sermon, "The promise is for you and for your children and for all who are far off, everyone whom the Lord our God calls to himself" (Acts 2:39). Cut to the quick by Peter's sermon, many believed and were baptized.

We are also told that converts brought their whole household under the covenant promises through baptism (Acts 16:14–15, 31; 1 Cor 1:16). The children of believers are holy, set apart by God's promise (1 Cor 7:14), although some will reject their birthright (Heb 12:16; cf. 6:1–9). There is, therefore, a birthright. Warnings against apostasy in the new covenant are grounded in the promises and threats that are found throughout the history of the one covenant of grace. The main argument is simple: those who belong to Christ are Abraham's spiritual offspring, heirs of the covenant promise (Rom 4:16–17; Gal 3:6–9, 14, 28; 4:30). The children of believers were heirs and therefore received God's sign and seal of his promise. This sacrament was circumcision in the old covenant, given to males only, and is baptism in the new covenant, received by males and females.

Responding to God's promise, parents—and indeed the whole church—vow to raise these children in the covenant. This shapes the entire outlook of the church in its ministry. There is the expectation that their children will come to profess faith publicly before the elders, and this will be ratified by their being welcomed to the Lord's Table.

There is also the other half of Peter's statement: "The promise is you and for your children *and for all who are far off,* everyone whom the Lord our God calls to himself." The church cannot be a secret society, closed in on itself. We cannot choose between a maintenance ministry and a missional ministry. Rather, the mission of the church is to announce and apply the promise to those within and those outside. We don't find in Acts two different ministries: one for adult conversions and another for "you and your children." Evangelization is for everyone, all the time, not just for special services. Yet evangelism requires preaching, baptism, and instruction in *everything* Christ taught and commanded (see Matt 28:18–20). This does not happen through extraordinary ministries but through the church's ordinary ministry.

While acknowledging surprising conversions (Luther's, for example), the Reformers saw conversion as a lifelong process of growing and deepening repentance and faith in Christ. This was not enough for the radical Protestants, though. A deeper question concerns our understanding of conversion. If you believe that genuine conversion is always a definable, radical, even datable moment, you will be inclined to look for obvious moments of revival that were radical breakthroughs on a wider scale. However, if you believe that the Spirit's work in conversion is mysterious and varies in its outward evidences from person to person, through the same ordinary ministry, you will be less likely to have lists of discernible experiences and evidences to which each must conform. You will rejoice with those who experience an obvious moment of conversion and also with those who come gradually to recognize that they belong to Christ. Furthermore, repentance and faith are not a one-time experience, but are part of a lifelong process that has ups and downs along the way. The most important thing to keep our eye on is not religious experience itself, but the faithful ministry of God's means of grace.

How Was Church Today?

Recall again Joe Queenan's clever description of Boomer aversion toward the ordinary.[46] The same is true of church. "How was church today?" In most times and places of the church, this would have been an unlikely question. In fact, the hearer might have been confused. Why? Because it's like asking how the meals at home have been this week or asking a farmer how the crops did this week. "How was the sermon?" "Was it a good service?" Same blank stare from the ancestors. In those days, churches didn't have to be rockin' it, nobody expected the preacher to hit it out of the park, and the service was, well, a service.

Now, that doesn't mean that what happens at church through these ordinary means in ordinary services of ordinary churches on ordinary weeks *is itself ordinary*. What happens is quite extraordinary indeed. First and foremost, God shows up. He judges and justifies, draws sinners and gathers his sheep to his Son by his Word and Spirit. He unites them to Christ, bathes them and feeds them, teaches and tends them along their pilgrim way. He expands his empire even as he deepens it. It is through this divinely ordained event that "the powers of the age to come" penetrate into the darkest crevices of this passing evil age (Heb 6:3–6).

So one way people might have responded in times past, at least in churches of the Reformation, would have been something like these expressions: "Well, it was one more nail in the coffin of the old Adam" or "God absolved me" or maybe something as simple as, "It's been good to understand the Gospel of John a little better over these past few months."

Once more, the marriage analogy is apt. Wrestling daily with whether they want to remain married to each other, many couples seeking counseling expect a *breakthrough*, preferably in the first session. Marital problems are treated like medical problems. "Make them go away." We can benefit from a good marriage conference, but then we return home and find ourselves back in the everydayness of actual marriage. It is there, in the daily grind, that we have to die to ourselves, loving and serving our closest neighbor.

A person may not share any responsibility for arthritis or kidney stones, and it is possible that the doctor can make it go away. However, marriage isn't like that. As in all relationships, we are both sinners and sinned against, perpetrators and victims — simultaneously. Furthermore, the expectation of "breakthroughs" reflects an impatience with — perhaps even misunderstanding of — marriage itself. If breakthroughs come at all, they arrive usually unbidden. Breakthroughs are what happen when you're expecting something else. When I hear — really hear — my wife say something for the first time that she has said over and over. When a wife does something unexpected for her husband and as a result they both end up taking fresh delight in each other. In other words, even breakthroughs usually come through ordinary acts.

These aren't breakthroughs that you go looking for; they're just things that happen in a marriage because you have two people being guided by God's good providence in spite of their sin. Now, add more sinners to the mix — first your own children. Then even more sinners — your local church. It is going to be tough, because, like us, these other people are still battling with selfishness and self-righteousness. But we're battling together. Nothing is more sanctifying than another person in our life. They are good at holding up mirrors, when we had quite different images of ourselves.

With the body of Christ, we only multiply the number of sinners involved. Yes, we are forgiven, justified, adopted. We are regenerated and are being conformed to the image of Christ. God's Word promises this and he ratifies it to each of us in baptism and Communion. Yet it's difficult to preserve the bond of unity when we are not only sinners but are so different in our backgrounds and interests. The Big Event — a conference, retreat, or concert — can sweep us off our feet. But the danger is that when we come back to our local church, we're disappointed. No more fireworks. It seems so ordinary.

The alternative to looking for breakthroughs is not passivity. In fact, it is relying on breakthroughs that makes us passive. We keep waiting for something to happen to us. We want the doctor to fix us and the counselor to fix our marriage and the pastor to fix any number of felt needs. But it is the ordinary disciplines and not the extraordinary breakthroughs that make a marriage. It is much easier to think—and even to say to our spouse, "Hey, let's go on an out-of-the-park vacation together, alone." That's where we'll have our breakthrough, right? So for the time being at least, we're off the hook. Until then, we can still be jerks to each other, spend the extra hour or two at the office, forget to ask how the doctor's visit went, and resent each other for "not meeting my needs." See how the search for the extraordinary actually undermines excellence—that which is true, good, and beautiful? How the passion for perpetual break-throughs actually makes us passive?

The same logic works for our life in the body of Christ. The summer camp, revival, new spiritual workout plan, or cultural-transformation strategy is equivalent to the "breakthrough" that short-term investors, couples, and Christians are looking for, but that actually keep them from becoming healthy, mature, and stable.

In the circles with which I'm most familiar, it isn't the summer camp or revival, but the parachurch ministry or conference that makes everyday faithfulness in a local church seem like a trip to the dentist. I encounter regularly professing Christians who lament their church situation, but did not rank "a solid church" at the top of their list when considering their move to a new city. They may attend the right conferences and read the right books, but they are a thorn in the side of their pastor and fellow members. Or perhaps they do not set aside the Lord's Day at all and fill the day with something other than the means of grace and the fellowship of the saints. But they blame the church for its failure to feed them.

Jesus Christ officially instituted the means of grace in clear and unmistakable terms: preaching the gospel, baptizing, and discipline—that is, teaching people to observe everything he commanded (Matt 28:19–20). In other words, it is what the Reformed confessions define as the "three marks of the church": no more, no fewer. There is no bait-and-switch. You don't start with "what people want" in order to get them to "what they need." The same means of grace that bring them in keep them in. We are passive recipients of Christ with all of his benefits, but this makes us active in everyday ways as we live with and love others.

Exercise

1. How does the church's attraction to The Next Big Thing reflect broader cultural influences?

2. Evangelicals are often suspicious of tradition, but is evangelicalism a tradition too? If so, in what ways — particularly, in ways that encourage new waves of extraordinary excitement?

3. Talk about revival. What are some of the different approaches to revival in our Anglo-American history? Are there any downsides to focusing on revival?

4. What would you say if someone asked you how church was this week? Reflect on your answers.

CHAPTER 5

ambition: how a vice became a virtue

Have you noticed how things that used to be considered vices are now regarded by many as virtues—and vice versa? The meaning of words changes over time. A century or two ago, a woman could be called "handsome," but a suitor would be ill-advised to do so today. Sometime around my high school years, the expression "bad"—used in the appropriate context—came to mean "good"; "wicked," in its most common use, now means "great." "Sick" means "wonderful." But these are merely colloquial expressions. It all depends on the context.

But then there are transformations not just in vocabulary but in values. "Restless" used to mean shifty, unreliable, even unstable. Today, however, to be restless is to be alive, always on the move, suspicious of authority, and discontent with standing still. Our idea of "ambition" has gone through a similar transformation.

The title of this chapter assumes that ambition itself is a vice: something wrong and sinful. For most people today, that is counterintuitive. But not that long ago it used to be a compliment to tell a person that he or she lacked ambition; today it is taken as a criticism. Ambition a vice? How can that be?

Of course, if by ambition we mean simply a drive or initiative in setting and reaching goals, there is nothing more natural to us as God's image-bearers. God created us in righteousness and holiness, to extend his reign to the ends of the earth. Glorifying and enjoying God was the object and goal that greeted Adam and Eve each morning, as they loved and served each other with energetic satisfaction. However, instead of leading his wife and his entire posterity in this "thanksgiving parade," Adam declared independence from his King. The immediate effects of his ambition were rivalry and self-assertion—first between Adam and Eve, and then between Cain and Abel. The rest, as they say, is history.

So too, however, is God's solution. In the fullness of time, the Father sent his Son. Where the first Adam sought to break free of his created rank and *ascend* to the throne of God, the last Adam—who is God in his very nature—left his throne and *descended* to our misery. "He … emptied himself, by taking the form of a servant, being born in the likeness of men. And being found in human form, he humbled himself by becoming obedient to the point of death, even death on a cross. Therefore God has highly exalted him and bestowed on him the name that is above every name, so that at the name of Jesus every knee should bow" (Phil 2:6–10). While the first Adam launched a "meet you at the top" philosophy of life, Jesus Christ says to the world, "I'll meet you at the bottom."

Our passion for life and achievement and our desire to strive toward a daring goal are essentially hardwired into us by God. What has changed since the fall is the direction of this drive. Unhinged from its proper object—God's glory and our neighbor's good—our love becomes self-focused; our holy passions become vicious, driving us away from God's approaching steps and away from each other. We're not living in the real world, the creation that God called into being and sustains by the word of his power, but in a make-believe world. We are living as though God and our neighbors were made for us. In other words, we are living *unnatural* lives—living as if we were or could become someone other than the image of God, created to love God and each other.

That is why the drive for achievement is no longer a virtue, why our pursuit of meaning and significance is so confusing and futile. This isn't new, as we learn from Ecclesiastes. From the first day of our fall into sin, the world that we imagine to exist and the selves that we presume to craft show themselves as empty shadows. Yet we keep the charade going because the reality is too great to bear, namely, that "all have sinned and fall short of the glory of God" and can only be justified by God "as a [free] gift" (Rom 3:23–24). This fallen condition expresses itself in idolatry and sexual immorality, where we even extinguish the light of nature.

Yet at its heart sin is the eclipse of thankfulness toward God (Rom 1:21). Why thankfulness? Because rather than seeing ourselves as self-creators who choose our own identity and purpose, the biblical worldview tells us that we are on the receiving end of our existence. We are beholden to someone else. Our life is a gift from God, not our own achievement. And our ingratitude is the clearest expression that we have idolized ourselves.

Ambition in Scripture

The Greek philosophers warned against ambition (*eritheia*). It did not mean drive or initiative. It meant putting oneself forward, as in an election, but in a spirit of rivalry that is not beneath resorting to unscrupulous tactics. A related term migrated into the world of medicine with *erythema*, "redness," which referred to the inflammation of the skin, like psoriasis. More generally, it could be used to refer to any disorder in the body—one's own body or the body politic.

But the Greeks did not see anything positive in its alternative. In fact, they regarded humility as the pose of a slave. Cultivating humility was not something they encouraged as a virtue for the nobler classes. This is why the incarnation of the Son of God in history constituted what one writer calls "a complete moral revolution." Our positive evaluation of humility is due entirely to the dawn of the new age in Christ.[47] A key passage for this is Philippians 2, where "self-sufficiency" founders. Where sinful humanity ascends to heaven in ambition, God himself descends in humility for us and for our salvation.

The apostle James reasons:

Who is wise and understanding among you? By his good conduct let him show his works in the meekness of wisdom. But if you have bitter jealousy and selfish ambition in your hearts, do not boast and be false to the truth. This is not the wisdom that comes down from above, but is earthly, unspiritual, demonic. For where jealousy and selfish ambition exist, there will be disorder and every vile practice. But the wisdom from above is first pure, then peaceable, gentle, open to reason, full of mercy and good fruits, impartial and sincere. And a harvest of righteousness is sown in peace by those who make peace. (Jas 3:13–18)

The Greek word translated "selfish ambition" in this passage is *eritheia*. In older English versions it is just "ambition." A modifier would have been considered redundant, like talking about "cold ice." Ambition was selfish by definition. The fact that our modern translations feel obliged to add "selfish" points out the change in our culture's evaluation of this attribute. Hence, James' observation: "For where jealousy and selfish ambition exist, there will be disorder and every vile practice." Ambition leads to disorder in the body.

Appealing to Christ's example of loving service to us, Paul exhorts the Philippians to humility and concord. "Do nothing from selfish ambition or conceit, but in humility count others more significant than yourselves. Let each of you look not only to his own interests, but also to the interests of others" (Phil 2:3–4).

Further, the terms "selfish ambition or conceit" in this passage are also translated from *eritheia* ("ambition") along with *kenodoxia* ("empty praise"; i.e., pretentiousness). Its next of kin are *philodoxia*, "love of praise," and *philautia*, "self-love." Paul is clearly telling his readers that the opposite of being of "one mind" is selfish ambition. Everyone has to be his own star in the show, breaking away from the consensus, blazing his own path. Not simply the celebrity leaders, but their adoring fans, are to be diagnosed with this cancer. "For people will be lovers of self, lovers of money, proud, arrogant, abusive, disobedient to their parents, ungrateful, unholy, heartless, unappeasable, slanderous, without self-control, brutal, not loving good, treacherous, reckless, swollen with conceit, lovers of pleasure rather than lovers of God" (2 Tim 3:2–4). Obviously, the warning includes people in the church: "having the appearance of godliness, but denying its power" (3:5).

For Paul, "enmity, strife, jealousy, fits of anger, rivalries, dissensions, divisions, envy" rank alongside drunken orgies and idolatry as "the works of the flesh" (Gal 5:19–21). The contrasting fruit of the Spirit include "love, joy, peace, patience, kindness, goodness, faithfulness, gentleness, self-control; against such things there is no law." "And those who belong to Christ Jesus," he adds, "have crucified the flesh with its passions and desires. If we live by the Spirit, let us also keep in step with the Spirit. Let us not become conceited, provoking one another, envying one another" (5:22–26).

The only instance in the English Bible where the notion of ambition is used positively is in Romans 15:20: "I make it my ambition to preach the gospel." But even here, the word Paul reaches for, *philotimoumenon*, simply means "strong desire." As he said at the beginning of the letter, he is "*eager [prothymon]* to preach the gospel" (Rom 1:15). In one other instance, Paul uses the verb in encouraging brotherly love "and to *aspire [philotimeisthai]* to live quietly, and to mind your own affairs, and to work with your hands, as we instructed you, so that you may walk properly before outsiders and be dependent on no one" (1 Thess 4:11–12). It is no small irony that Paul encourages an aspiration—even ambition—to mind our own business and fulfill our ordinary callings.

Especially in Romans 12 and 1 Corinthians 12, Paul draws on a familiar analogy to describe the church as a system of interrelated and interdependent parts with Christ as the head. In this body, each member plays an important role, regardless of the degree of honor or prestige. An arthritic joint in one finger causes the whole body to suffer. The hand doesn't exist for itself, but for the body. Every member has something that the whole body needs. "To each is given the manifestation of the Spirit for the common good" (1 Cor 12:7). After listing some of these gifts, the apostle reasons:

> If the foot should say, "Because I am not a hand, I do not belong
> to the body," that would not make it any less a part of the body....

> If the whole body were an eye, where would be the sense of hearing?... But as it is, God has arranged the members in the body, each one of them, as he chose....
>
> The eye cannot say to the hand, "I have no need of you," nor again the head to the feet, "I have no need of you." On the contrary, the parts of the body that seem to be weaker are indispensable, and on those parts of the body that we think less honorable we bestow the greater honor, and our unpresentable parts are treated with greater modesty. (1 Cor 12:15–23)

Paul then makes the point: "that there may be no division in the body, but that the members may have the same care for one another. If one member suffers, all suffer together; if one member is honored, all rejoice together" (1 Cor 12:25–26).

This isn't every person for himself, but all for one and one for all: Christ for us and then us for each other. It may not make any sense to people around us, but when a brother or sister falls down, we do not keep running, much less demean them, but turn back to pick the person up. If necessary, we carry him or her to the finish line. In the old age that is passing away, under the reign of sin and death, I didn't shoulder other people *or* let them carry me. In the dawn of the age to come, however, I am free to bear their burdens and to allow them to bear mine (Gal 6:2). As my generation used to sing, "He ain't heavy, he's my brother." "Above all," Peter exhorts, "keep loving one another earnestly, since love covers a multitude of sins" (1 Pet 4:8). Peter isn't saying that our loving acts atone for sin. Far from it! Peter's astonishing point is that love hides the faults of others rather than making a spectacle of them.

Christians should be some of the most conflicted people in the world. It is far simpler to be dead to God and to live for oneself. But Christians must struggle against their selfish ambition because they are alive to God in Christ Jesus, and the indwelling Spirit turns on the lights to enable them to see their sin. The old Adam in us thinks we're crazy. Thinking more highly of others than you do of yourself is not the way the world works. Follow that logic and you'll be left in the dust, he counsels. Love is fine in the abstract, but how can you love someone without doing some sort of cost-benefit analysis? There is a calculus here: you have to balance community and autonomy. But both of these ideals are motivated by the selfish horizon of this present age.

Contra the wisdom of this age, Paul tells us that the body of Christ is not just a voluntary association for realizing my dream of "belonging" or a place where I can assert my unique qualities. Christ's body is not a stage for my performance, but an organism into which I've been inserted by the Spirit, by a miracle of grace.

Envy fuels a restless discontent. Selfish ambition and lazy self-loathing differ only in the way they act on this envy. One must aspire aggressively to something more than his or her ordinary place and gifting—or acquiesce in resentful passivity toward the rest of the body. A "toe" aspiring to a "higher" status, like a hand—or even the head—abandons the calling for which God prepared and gifted it. Discontent, perhaps even envious and resentful, refuses to take its assigned place where its function is crucial for the whole body.

If we stick closely to the biblical terms for it, ambition is folly, for we will take God's gift of godly aspiration and fashion them into weapons of self-interest. "Ultimately, it's we ourselves who hold ambition hostage," notes Dave Harvey, "and we'll drop godly drives if something more attractive shows up—and in the process, the right kind of dreams die."[48] Ambition is an empty pursuit, because none of us is truly the master of our fate and the captain of our soul. We cannot live up to our own Facebook profile or the expectations that have been placed on us by others. When we do try to disengage ourselves from the ties that bind, the whole body suffers. As we have seen above, especially from Paul's exhortations, ambition is bound up with rivalry, factions, jealousy, envy, and even fits of rage. When we are ambitious, each of us campaigns for the office of emperor. In the process, we're tearing Christ's body, our homes, our workplaces, and our society to pieces.

Melted Wings and How a Vice Became a Virtue

Just a couple of decades before Christ's birth, the Roman poet Ovid popularized the tragic tale of Icarus. After falling out of favor with his ruler, King Midos, the master architect and craftsman Daedalus found himself imprisoned in a labyrinth that he had constructed for the king's enemies. His son, Icarus, was condemned to share his fate. One day, Daedalus made wings from feathers and wax and the father and son took flight. Soaring over the islands and fishing boats, they reveled not only in their liberation but in the freedom of the skies. Yet Icarus wanted something more: to ascend to the sun itself. Ovid related the lad's mournful demise:

> By this time Icarus began to feel the joy
> Of beating wings in air and steered his course
> Beyond his father's lead: all the wide sky
> Was there to tempt him as he steered toward heaven.
> Meanwhile the heat of sun struck at his back
> And where his wings were joined, sweet-smelling fluid
> Ran hot that once was wax. His naked arms
> Whirled into wind; his lips, still calling out
> His father's name, were gulfed in the dark sea.
> And the unlucky man, no longer father,
> Cried, "Icarus, where are you, Icarus,
> Where are you hiding, Icarus, from me?"
> Then as he called again, his eyes discovered
> The boy's torn wings washed on the climbing waves.
> He damned his art, his wretched cleverness,
> Rescued the body and placed it in a tomb,
> And where it lies the land's called Icarus.[49]

In a recent study, William Casey King traces the transformation of "ambition" from vice to virtue.[50] Since antiquity, ambition was associated with pride, and Christian thinkers underscored its destructive power. Ambrose, the fourth-century bishop of Milan, called ambition a "hidden plague."[51] Augustine warned of the *libido dominandi*—the craving to dominate, that is, a corruption of the good stewardship that God entrusted to humanity. Thomas Aquinas identified ambition unequivocally as a sin.

The Protestant Reformers concurred. In fact, ambition was a frequent target in their writings and sermons. They discerned it in the papacy, in the radical sects that sought to turn everything upside down, in the rising merchant class, and among the rising nation builders. They also lamented its rapacious entrance into their own circles.

In his "Anatomy of the World" (1611), poet and preacher John Donne pointed to the clouds on the horizon: "And new philosophy calls all in doubt."

> 'Tis all in pieces, all coherence gone;
> All just supply, and all Relation;
> Prince, Subject, Father, Son, are things forgot,
> For every man alone thinks he hath got
> To be a Phoenix, and that then can be
> None of that kind, of which he is, but he.[52]

Returning to King's survey, we discover the many references to ambition in the notes of the Geneva Bible, which shaped the literary imagination of Shakespeare, Milton, and Marlowe. One might also add that Milton and Marlowe also invoked the tale of Icarus. The ambitious villain is Shakespeare's Macbeth, Milton's Lucifer, and Marlowe's Doctor Faustus.

Shakespeare offers his own definition of Hamlet's ambition: "dreams indeed are ambition, for the very substance of the ambitious is merely the shadow of a dream.... I hold ambition of so airy and light a quality that it is but a shadow's shadow."[53] Yet we feel ourselves closer to Nietzsche's interpretation, which he felt sure Shakespeare himself must have intended:

> He who is really possessed by raging ambition beholds this its image [Macbeth] with joy; and if the hero perishes by his passion this precisely is the sharpest spice in the hot draught of this joy. Can the poet have felt otherwise? How royally, and not at all

like a rogue, does [t]his ambitious man pursue his course from the moment of his great crime![54]

Nietzsche's fanciful redescription is a fatal marker of the cultural turning point in our evaluation of this vice.

Drawing on passages like Romans 12 and 1 Corinthians 12, Reformed preachers taught that limitations are healthy—both for us and for others. They encouraged excellence and opened new doors of literacy and learning that were previously unavailable to many, including women. There were new opportunities for improving one's lot in life. Yet they discouraged "wandering stars," as Calvin often referred to the restless souls who were never content with their calling and circumstances in life.

In his providence, God has given to each of us specific gifts, inclinations, talents, and opportunities. We are not unlimited. Our future is not "whatever we want it to be," and we are not able to become "whatever we wish." Yet all of this is for our good—and the good of others. The gifts and opportunities we have been given are to be used not merely for private advancement, but for the public good. And this is why we all need each other. In society, every sort of calling is needed for the commonwealth. So too in the church, even a little finger cannot be hurt without the whole body aching. The priesthood of all believers did not mean that every believer held a special office in the church. There is still a proper order for the complete harmony and growth of the body.

Wherever this type of piety spread, there was a sense that the diversity of stations in life was something to celebrate rather than eliminate. Most of the verses in the children's hymn "All Things Bright and Beautiful" magnify God's glory in creating so much diversity in colors, plants, climate, terrain, and geography. Then there is verse 3:

The rich man in his castle,
The poor man at his gate,
God made them high and lowly,
And ordered their estate.[55]

It is worth noting that this verse has been eliminated from many modern hymnals as contrary to the egalitarian spirit. But what about "the poor man at his gate"? Are we basically telling such brothers and sisters that their life is an embarrassment? That they have failed to make something of themselves? Are we implying that they are victims of oppression when it may be just as plausible that they are living happy and healthy lives, participating more deeply in the exchange of gifts in their own circle? And do we assume that one's social status is determinative for his or her place in the body of Christ? That their gifts and callings are not good enough to supply what the rest of us lack?

We're called to be children, students, and friends; then also to be spouses and parents, employers and employees, neighbors and citizens. We are also called to be members of a local expression of Christ's body. All of these callings keep us within bounds, to be sure. Who can deny that being married and having children is being "tied down"?

We all want to live for ourselves and yet be cared for, to have authority without responsibility, to be beneficiaries of the gift exchange without being benefactors. There's nothing new there. What is somewhat new is that this consummate hubris is seen increasingly not as an evil to be repented of, but a basic human right.

People who are perfectly content — truly happy — being janitors or gardeners are encouraged to become dissatisfied and restless. They should aim for the stars. Everyone should strive to work his or her way from the mail room to the boardroom. Even to question that, and to value neighbors simply for who they are in the civil body as well as the body of Christ, is considered condescending. Actually, though, isn't it *less* condescending to recognize the value of each person and his or her role in society and in Christ's body?

Democracy has opened the door to new opportunities, but it has also created a new kind of elitism, one that is based not on inherited position but on what people have "made of themselves." In some ways this is even more condescending than the aristocratic feudalism that at least had a sense of noblesse oblige — that is, the obligation of the higher for the lower as well as the lower for the higher. Like a fever that drives one mad, ambition causes one to take himself or herself out of the circulation of this gift-giving.

What's striking in the literature from Reformed and Puritan pens are the numerous warnings directed to rulers and aspiring rulers, including the new class of upwardly mobile businesspeople and politicians. Kings heard sermons reminding them that they were given their calling by God's providence for the common good, not for private enrichment or power, and that he pulled the mighty down as well as raised them up.

With Francis Bacon at the beginning of the seventeenth century, ambition came to be seen, not as another sin to confess, but as inevitable human lust to be channeled into socially constructive ways. Ambition was still seen as a vice, but as more of an illness than a sin. What do you do in that case? You inject antibodies to fight a bacterial infection, fighting fire with fire. Writing during the London plague, Bacon had a ready analogy: sometimes poisons, taken in the proper measure, are the only antidote.[56] As James Madison put it in Federalist No. 51, "Ambition must be made to counteract ambition."[57]

Doubtless, explorers and colonizers were driven by nobler motives as well, but it was becoming clear that ambition could be domesticated. Many came to believe that it could be harnessed "for God and country," while not failing to bring wealth and fame to those swift and sure of foot.

Today, the habits of explorers, conquerors, and experimenters have become the values of the common person. Everyone is meant to break away from the herd and to become a phoenix rising from the ashes. The spirit of ambition is expressed in the rousing sentiment of General George S. Patton: "I do not fear failure. I only fear the 'slowing up' of the engine inside of me which is pounding, saying, 'Keep going, someone must be on top, why not you?'" Perhaps it is most obvious in the entertainment industry, with TV programs like *The Apprentice, Project Runway, Master Chef,* and *Survivor*. The most obvious lesson is to do anything you need to in order to get ahead.

The aspiration to achieve has made America the land of opportunity. Yet it also comes at a price. Today, personal achievement is valued as an end in itself. The character it forms assumes that possibilities are endless, resources infinite; that limitations on personal choice are intrinsically evil, that everyone should go to college and become a successful businessperson, engineer, lawyer, doctor, or other professional. Where it becomes *normal*, success thus defined becomes *expected*. Converted from vice to virtue, ambition was spurred by the trophy awarded to the high achievers. But now every kid receives a trophy just for showing up. We're all extraordinary now. Every American is entitled to the best of everything. Ironically, the democratizing of ambition is undermining genuine distinction and excellence. For those who fall short of the glory of the American dream, the fate can be as tragic as it was for Icarus.

Ambition is a focal point for something that creates within us — especially in our younger years — a tension between self and community. "Ambition drives people forward; relationships and community, by imposing limits, hold people back," writes Emily Esfahani Smith. "Which is more important?" Her article in *The Atlantic* argues that "relationships are more important than ambition: there's more to life than leaving home."[58]

It is not surprising that Friedrich Nietzsche, the modern propagandist for the will to power, considered Christianity the great inhibitor of noble ambition. Nietzsche believed that the cross is a symbol of an entire religion's devotion to mediocrity, justifying a passive acquiescence to power and the herd instinct. "This God has degenerated into a staff for the weak, the god of the poor, the sinners, the sick par excellence." The poor German became "a 'sinner,' stuck in a cage, imprisoned among all sorts of terrible concepts … fully of suspicion against all that was still strong and happy. In short, a 'Christian.' "[59] "A god who died for our sins; redemption through faith; resurrection after death — all these are counterfeits of true Christianity for which that disastrous wrong-headed fellow Paul must be held responsible."[60]

Never known for nuance on such subjects, Nietzsche was reacting against the suffocating moralism of bourgeois liberal pietism. He failed to recognize the life-affirming and world-embracing message of biblical Christianity. He missed the point that Christ's death was not a symbol of anything, but an unrepeatable rescue operation in history. He seems not to have understood that Jesus never acquiesced to power. Ironically, as his disciples argued over rank in the kingdom (Luke 22:24–30) and Jesus nipped Peter's ambition in the bud by foretelling his betrayal (22:31–34), Jesus—who actually possessed all power—told them that he was actively embracing his impending death: "For I tell you that this Scripture must be fulfilled in me: 'And he was numbered with the transgressors'" (22:37; cf. Mark 10:45; John 15:12–13). Even then, "they said, 'Look, Lord, here are two swords.' And he said to them, 'It is enough'" (22:38).

Earlier, Jesus had told a crowd that he will *lay down* his life. "No one takes it from me, but I lay it down of my own accord. I have authority to lay it down, and I have authority to take it up again." Yet even he does so not as Nietzsche's "Superman," but says, "This charge I have received from my Father" (John 10:17–18). "Do you not know that I have authority to release you and authority to crucify you?" Pilate asked Jesus at his trial. "Jesus answered him, 'You would have no authority over me at all unless it had been given you from above" (19:10–11).

Yet Jesus does this out of submission to his Father and his love for us. Here is one man—the only man in history—who could truly have had the world at his feet. He could have turned Pilate and his court to ash by a mere word. Not for a moment was he a powerless victim. On the contrary, with Christ a new power—a power of forgiveness, love, and mercy—entered this world filled with aspiring gods who live disillusioned and vacuous lives. By enduring the cross, he was raised victorious, leading liberated captives in his train as he ascended to the throne of all power in heaven and on earth.

Furthermore, *we* are crucified with Christ only to be raised with him in newness of life. The cross didn't have the last word over Jesus, and therefore it doesn't over us.

For Nietzsche, as for many in the West today, power is

synonymous with ambition. Those who embrace this simplistic choice are to be pitied. They know nothing of the power of love, forgiveness, care, and sacrifice. Therefore, even after misunderstandings are corrected, the basic thrust of Nietzsche's hostile reaction remains valid to anyone for whom the idol of ambition remains well-polished in the temple.

Death and Resurrection, Not a Makeover

It seems obvious enough that selfish ambition at the least entertains bad company in the Bible. It is the spirit that corrupted Lucifer, the erstwhile angel of light in God's royal court; it is the venom that filled Adam's heart with swollen pride, and the vain conceit that erected the Tower of Babel. Selfish ambition is the self-love that seeks to ascend beyond the skies in a solo flight, away from God and the community of fellow creatures.

As far as Scripture is concerned, *passionate drives* can be godly or ungodly, but *ambition* cannot be channeled into good directions or harnessed for noble ends. It is the heart of the sinful self who must die and be raised with a new identity, a new name, a new hope, and a new way of existing — not in oneself, but "in Christ."

It is not simply that a Judeo-Christian culture has been warped by worldly values. After all, what does one expect from the world — even in a more church-friendly version of it? The real tragedy is that in some ways churches have themselves helped to facilitate these transformations, however unintentionally. The ambition of explorers and imperial churches of yesteryear could be cloaked in pious rhetoric — "for the glory of God and the extension of his kingdom."

Ambition — even in the older sense, as the desire to rise above all others — can be harnessed for the call to be a spiritual superhero. We see this tendency today in the way we hold up "celebrities who know the Lord" as icons. What would it say to our youth group if, instead of inviting the former NFL star, we had a couple visit who had been married for forty-five years to talk honestly about the ups and downs of growing together in Christ? What if we held up those "ordinary" examples of humble and faithful service over the worldly success stories?

The challenge here is that we have been trained to read even the Bible as a catalog of heroes to emulate. Moses is the great model of leadership, Joshua is the ideal warrior, and we should "dare to be a Daniel," as the old hymn exhorts. This is a little odd, when you actually read the narratives and discover that Abraham, Noah, Moses, David, and all the rest were ordinary sinners like the rest of us who had received an extraordinary calling. They fell short of that calling, but God was faithful. And they too needed a Savior—and this is the central plot unfolding in Scripture. In our ambition, we trip over the central character and the central meaning of the whole story.

A. W. Tozer put his finger on this problem:

> The new cross does not slay the sinner, it redirects him. It gears him into a cleaner and jollier way of living and saves his self-respect. To the self-assertive it says, "Come and assert yourself for Christ." To the egotist it says, "Come and do your boasting in the Lord." To the thrill-seeker it says, "Come and enjoy the thrill of Christian fellowship." The Christian message is slanted in the direction of the current vogue in order to make it acceptable to the public.[61]

Ambition is ambition, no matter what package it comes in. There are actually leaders today who identify themselves as apostles, founders, or otherwise pioneers extraordinaire of the church. While they dismiss the checks and balances of older and wiser forms of church government, they end up claiming the throne for themselves.

Familiar terminology may still be used, but its meaning has changed because its entire frame of reference has become secularized. Where the biblical message calls us to the cross, to die to self and to be raised in Christ, the new message calls the old Adam to an improved self, empowered to fulfill more easily his own life project. The new evangelism negotiates a contract with the sinner rather than announcing God's judgment on the sinner and the good news of a covenant of grace. Thus, the church becomes another service provider governed by the autonomous choices of consumers, simply perpetuating the illusion of self-sovereignty that leads to death.

The point of this brief survey is to remind ourselves that our habits are not simply shaped by our beliefs; our beliefs are also shaped by what we — not merely as individuals, but as a society evolving over generations — have come to accept and desire as good, true, and beautiful.[62] Ultimately, we have to decide which story we truly believe.

Even good things can be corrupted when we become curved in on ourselves. And that's why we must die. In the true version of the story, the gospel, we learn that we all die in order to be raised as a living member of the new creation: justified, adopted, raised with Christ, and "seated ... with him in the heavenly places" (Eph 2:6–7). We forget that we can't be happy by looking for happiness; we can't be successful by aiming at success; we can't be passionate by trying to be more passionate. We need someone other than ourselves to love, desire, and trust. We can't invent or reinvent ourselves. We do not choose our own nature from a supermarket of unlimited options. That is a fable we keep telling ourselves as we fly with waxen wings toward the sun.

Exercise

1. How does Scripture define and evaluate ambition? Identify some key character traits that cluster around this vice?
2. How has the myth of Icarus played out in history, and how have Christians responded to it in previous generations?
3. Is ambition something that we can harness for positive ends? What is meant by the point that what we need is death, not a makeover?

CHAPTER 6

practicing what we preach: no more super-apostles

The United States was born in a revolt against royal tyranny. Colonial flags bore slogans like "Don't tread on me" and "We serve no sovereigns here." The alternative was not anarchy, but a settled constitution for a republic that would be ruled by laws rather than by human beings. Yet the protest against earthly sovereigns bled into a religion of self-sufficiency before God. No longer pawns of royal and aristocratic ambition, each citizen was now free to pursue his or her own ambition as long as it did not interfere with the ambitions of others.

The story of American independence is a stirring chapter in the history of nations. Yet Christians cannot fail to appreciate with regret the extent to which selfish ambition — disguised as liberty — has infected the church. After all, we still serve a sovereign — the King of kings. It is he who has delivered us from the hands of our enemies at the cost of his own blood, and it is he who has delivered his constitution to us through the hands of his apostles. It is he who continues his reign through fallible ministers, elders, and deacons. He rules to save and he saves to rule. If we are living as if there were no king and everyone is free to do what is right in their own eyes, then we are not living in the church that Christ has established.

A democratic view of the church is a rebellion against God and his Messiah. The American colonists declared independence, won it, and therefore created a constitution for a nation "of the people, by the people, for the people." However, God created us as dependent image bearers, liberated us one-sidedly from death and hell, and therefore has the sole right to determine the constitution for his holy nation.

As we saw in the previous chapter, ambition unleashes the war of all against all, where each of us becomes a little emperor. Left unchecked, we come to the place where we cannot submit to anyone or anything. We alone choose what to believe, how to live, and what sort of church appeals to us. But since not everyone will be as successful in fulfilling their ambitions, the cream will inevitably rise to the top and those most gifted at appealing to (and manipulating) our choices will become our de facto rulers. Apart from our Servant King, who reigns through his ordained means, constitution, and offices, we will be at the mercy of self-appointed despots who rule according to their own whim.

Between these diverse poles lies the vast spectrum of actual life in the church.

Paul and the "Super-Apostles"

It is hardly surprising when prosperity evangelists fall into scandals of various sorts or when apostles of self-esteem become a little too fond of themselves. The real tragedy is the extent to which ambition and even avarice are tolerated—even cloaked in pious expressions—in more traditional circles.

We can take some comfort in knowing that we are not alone in dealing with these problems. Even among the disciples themselves, the fever entered the camp:

> A dispute also arose among them, as to which of them was to be regarded as the greatest. And he said to them, "The kings of the Gentiles exercise lordship over them, and those in authority over them are called benefactors. But not so with you. Rather, let the greatest among you become as the youngest, and the leader as one who serves. For who is the greater, one who reclines at table or one who serves? Is it not the one who reclines at table? But I am among you as the one who serves." (Luke 22:24–27)

The thrones in his kingdom are not *won* by ambitious men, Jesus said, but "I assign to you, as my Father assigned to me, a kingdom, that you may eat and drink at my table in my kingdom and sit on thrones judging the twelve tribes of Israel" (Luke 22:29–30). Similarly, Paul says that different spiritual gifts were assigned to each believer by the Spirit, all of grace (Eph 4:7).

Clustering around favorite teachers was a danger even in the apostolic era. Disagreement and division over basic doctrine is always tragic, but often necessary (1 Cor 11:19). However, most divisions — then and ever since — are provoked by ambitious people who sow discord in order to draw disciples after themselves (Rom 16:17; 1 Cor 1:10; Titus 3:10; Jude 19).

Paul was wrestling with this even in the churches that he planted. Some of those who at first embraced his gospel message with joy became bored with its simplicity. Surely there must be something more. That is where the "super-apostles" came into the picture. These persuasive speakers claimed to know secrets far greater than the apostles, especially Paul, had revealed. Just look at Paul! Weak and unappealing, without flowery oratory, Paul hardly looked the part of a divine ambassador. How easy it is to draw people away from the simplicity of the gospel with smooth talk!

> For if someone comes and proclaims another Jesus than the one we proclaimed, or if you receive a different spirit from the one you received, or if you accept a different gospel from the one you accepted, you put up with it readily enough. Indeed, I consider that I am not in the least inferior to these super-apostles. Even if I am unskilled in speaking, I am not so in knowledge; indeed, in every way we have made this plain to you in all things. (2 Cor 11:4–6)

Yet Paul is not deterred from his message or mission:

> And what I am doing I will continue to do, in order to undermine the claim of those who would like to claim that in their boasted mission they work on the same terms as we do. For such men are false apostles, deceitful workmen, disguising themselves as apostles of Christ. (2 Cor 11:12–13)

The apostle to the Gentiles knew that he would not be emulated for his personal charisma or leadership qualities or creative strategies. Actually, the naturally gifted and self-promoting "super-apostles" scored high marks on that exam. "For what we proclaim is not ourselves, but Jesus Christ as Lord, with ourselves as your servants for Jesus' sake. . . . But we have this treasure in jars of clay, to show that the surpassing power belongs to God and not to us" (2 Cor 4:5, 7). It's the message, not the messenger.

So Paul exhorts the Corinthians, "Be imitators of me, as I am of Christ" (1 Cor 11:1). But the real heroes—the people we should look up to, like Paul—are not the ones who set out to be heroes in the first place. Paul believed that even the apostles are merely witnesses to Christ, who is building his church. "What is then Apollos? What is Paul?" They are simply servants through whom people believed the gospel (1 Cor 3:5). We need more ordinary ministers who, like Paul, not only say this but act as if it's true.

In 1 Timothy the apostle draws an intriguing connection between false doctrine and ungodly ambition. To follow up this connection, in chapter 5 he gives instructions on proper order, offices, and discipline in the church. Then in chapter 6 he encourages each person to embrace his or her calling in society and in the church with contentment:

> Teach and urge these things. If anyone teaches a different doctrine and does not agree with the sound words of our Lord Jesus Christ and the teaching that accords with godliness, he is puffed up with conceit and understands nothing. He has an unhealthy craving for controversy and for quarrels about words, which produce envy, dissension, slander, evil suspicions, and constant friction among people who are depraved in mind and deprived of the truth, imagining that godliness is a means of gain. (1 Tim 6:2b–5)

The two sides are clear here. Proper church order stands in marked contrast to the self-made and self-authorized teacher who gathers admirers with their checkbooks. The church that Christ is building and Timothy is called to serve has checks and balances. It's not "Timothy's church" or "Timothy's ministry," but Christ's, built on the foundation of the apostles.

Paul stresses the point that "I did not receive [the gospel] from any man, nor was I taught it, but I received it through a revelation of Jesus Christ" (Gal 1:12). After this revelation, he adds, "I did not immediately consult with anyone" — not even the apostles in Jerusalem; only after three years in Arabia and then back to Damascus did he visit Peter and stay with him for two weeks (1:16 – 18). Eventually, this former persecutor was accepted by all of the apostles in Jerusalem as called directly by Jesus, as they were.

Yet Paul's calling is qualitatively different from Timothy's, and you see this in the contrast between the passage in Galatians 1 and the exhortation he gives to his apprentice. He tells Timothy that he is simply to pass on to others what he has received from Paul the apostle, to keep the deposit rather than add to it, to teach it to other men who will carry on the work. The super-apostles boasted of a "higher knowledge" (*gnōsis*) than the apostles' doctrine, seeking to reinvent a gospel more "relevant" to Greeks. But Paul warns, "O Timothy, guard the deposit entrusted to you. Avoid the irreverent babble and contradictions of what is falsely called 'knowledge,' for by professing it some have swerved from the faith" (1 Tim 6:20 – 21). Unlike the apostles, Timothy is not called immediately and directly by Jesus Christ, but through the ministry of the church. He is answerable to the presbytery — or council of elders — that ordained him (4:14). Timothy is not an apostle; he is serving in the vanguard of the ordinary ministry that will continue after the extraordinary ministry of the apostles.

Notice again the contrast we have encountered before. On one side is the self-ordained "wandering star," who gathers fans eager to hear the latest thing, especially if it flatters their own self-love (2 Tim 3:1 – 9). Ranging beyond his competence, he introduces new speculations that bring controversy and rivalry. He is all over the map, taking hapless victims with him on his ambitious journey toward the sun.

Then there is Timothy, who is an ordinary minister accountable to ordinary elders, who is simply supposed to "guard the good deposit entrusted to [him]" (2 Tim 1:14) and "fight the good fight of faith" (1 Tim 6:12) with "steadfastness" (6:11). The church is apostolic, not because it claims a continuing apostolic office, but because it proclaims and guards the apostolic doctrine and discipline. It's not his amazing charisma, leadership skills, or even out-of-the-park teaching ability that matters. In fact, the more he tries to distinguish himself, the more division he will bring to the church. Rather, without ever crossing his fingers behind his back, he is called simply to remain faithful to his ordination vows: "the good confession in the presence of many witnesses" (1 Tim 6:12). In his instruction to Timothy, then, Paul lays out the contrast by emphasizing the need to be content with the ordinary means of grace that God has provided through the church, not giving into senseless desires, youthful lusts, and selfish ambition.

What is the takeaway from this? What does it say to us today? I believe it means that we desperately need more Timothys and a lot fewer would-be Pauls in the church. We need to wean ourselves away from identifying particular churches as "So-And-So's church," from identifying the church with gifted speakers and charismatic leaders. I once heard an associate minister at a prominent church say that his entire mission was "to protect Pastor X's ministry." While this may sound humble, it is arrogant for us to speak of the church and the ministry as belonging to anyone other than Jesus Christ.

Even in Reformed circles to which I belong, there can be a tendency to gather around teachers, to invoke famous authors from the past against living pastors and elders who teach and watch over us, and to prefer theology conferences and teaching media (yes, even the White Horse Inn) to the ordinary, week-in-and-week-out instruction in God's Word.

Others advance a "Moses Model of Ministry." Beginning as a rebellion against formal structures and church offices (even membership), such groups eventually evolve into a virtually papal hierarchy. Still others identify their leader as an apostle, and internal criticism is rebuffed with the warning, "Touch not the Lord's anointed." Some of these teachers may be closer to Paul in their message, but they are closer to the super-apostles in their ministry.

All of these models overlook the qualitative difference between the *extraordinary ministry* of the apostles and the *ordinary ministry* of those who followed them. There are no living prophets or apostles today—in Rome, in Texas, in California, or anywhere else. Their extraordinary ministry laid the foundation (1 Cor 3:10–11; Eph 2:20) on which the ordinary ministers build up the church (1 Cor 3:12–15; Eph 4:11–14).

Many examples could be drawn from history to make the point that people we consider heroes (like Paul) became "heroic" by seeking someone or something other than heroism. Their success is due to the extent to which they attached people to Christ instead of themselves. It is ordinary needs of others that keeps them going, against all odds. They are not interested in making headlines for a cause, but in particular people with whom they come into contact. Whatever success they attained was the result of countless decisions and acts that many of us would consider too ordinary to keep our interest. Perpetual innovation and a craving for success itself would never have allowed these people to become who, by God's grace, they were.

The rest of us are people whom one will never hear or read about in the newspaper or the annals of church history. We know less about Timothy and nothing about most of the faithful shepherds who have passed that sacred baton from generation to generation. Yet even today many of these pastors and elders are going about their daily tasks that are no less mundane and no less important for those around them. They are doing precisely what they are supposed to do, right where they are.

In Matthew 25:31–46, Jesus speaks about the separation of the sheep and the goats at the last judgment. Two things stand out in this glimpse that Jesus gives us of the day of the Lord. First, notice the works that the sheep did (and the goats failed to do). Anticipating the approaching persecution, Jesus says that the sheep visited their brothers and sisters in prison, gave them water, and clothed them. It is not exactly the global magic that we would expect, but these *ordinary* kindnesses reveal their faith.

The second thing we should notice is that the goats question where they may have seen Jesus doing these things.[63] Now these are the sorts of things that the world might take seriously. Yet Jesus says, "Depart from me." They skipped the little things and took refuge in their own spiritual ambition. By contrast, when Jesus commends the sheep for their seemingly slight and invisible faithfulness, instead of replying in self-defense, "Lord did we not...?" they reply, "Lord, when did we...?" The sheep do not even remember the deeds for which they are commended.

Idolizing Our Leaders

The writer to the Hebrews exhorts, "Remember your leaders, those who spoke to you the word of God. Consider the outcome of their way of life, and imitate their faith" (Heb 13:7). So there is respect—even reverence—for their office and the weighty ministry that they carry out. But the focus is on the word of God that they spoke, the outcome of their steadfastness, and their faith—not on their personality or skills as such.

As late as the fourth century, theologians of such stature as Jerome and Ambrose could point out that presbyters (pastors and elders) were "all alike of equal rank" in the apostolic era.[64] "Before attachment to persons in religion was begun at the instigation of the devil, the churches were governed by the common consent of the elders."[65]

In the East, church leaders warned that any assertion of one bishop's primacy over all others would constitute an act of schism. In fact, the sixth-century bishop of Rome, Gregory the Great, expressed offense at being addressed by a bishop as "universal pope":

> ... a word of proud address that I have forbidden.... None of my predecessors ever wished to use this profane word ["universal"]....
> But I say it confidently, because whoever calls himself "universal bishop" or wishes to be so called, is in his self-exaltation Antichrist's precursor, for in his swaggering he sets himself before the rest.[66]

Tragically, Gregory's successors didn't follow his advice. Eventually, they did claim this title of "proud address," and others besides.

But leadership problems are hardly unique to the Roman Catholic church. Ironically, radical Protestant sects are typically born as an eruption of supposed liberation from formal offices and structures of mutual accountability and quickly cool into corporations with a charismatic figure calling the shots. In charismatic and Pentecostal circles, successive waves of revival—characterized as "fresh moves of the Spirit"—disturb steady growth with perpetual Moses figures and new apostles. "I am of Paul," "I am Apollos," "I am of Peter": this rivalry becomes as obvious in Protestant circles as in Roman Catholicism today.

Even in the first Great Awakening, a pastor who did not support the movement and encourage members to attend the meetings was suspect. Many pastors were for that reason denounced as lukewarm or even unconverted. Every purported revival leaves rivalries and factions in its wake, with parties divided over which leader is truly the Lord's anointed. Even in circles closer to my own, I hear noted pastors identifying themselves as a leader of a "tribe." According to the apostles, tribalism is the sinful disorder that follows in ambition's wake.

In Lutheran and Reformed churches, we are divided less over movements and leaders than by schools and scholars. At their best, our Reformed and Presbyterian churches unite around the biblical teaching summarized by the ecumenical creeds, confessions, and catechisms and require mutual submission of equal pastors and elders to local and broader assemblies. Individual officers do not make unilateral decisions; they are made by common consent as a body. Nevertheless, we find it so easy to impose on each other our own extra-confessional positions and, especially in the internet age, find it easier sometimes to prosecute pastors in blogs than in these face-to-face assemblies. For some (both officers and other members), no church seems to satisfy their personal ambition, under the cloak of doctrinal purity. Regardless of public vows of membership they have made, they break fellowship and ride off into the sunset—perhaps leaving intentional landmines of dissension to explode after they are gone.

There is something distinctive—and, to some extent, distinctively American—about the penchant for rivalries and factions. It is not even the disputed views that interest us as much as it is the line drawing. As C. S. Lewis observed, we all want to be in the "inner ring," like the cool kids at school. It's collective narcissism. We love to divide over various formulations and to form caucuses. Blogging only adds fuel to the fire. Something happens even to decent people when they can hide behind the computer screen. Issues worth discussing and even debating soon congeal into parties. At that point, good conversations are thwarted by self-appointed umpires who censure the slightest departure from their own opinions.

Increasingly, we prefer to lynch fellow shepherds via social media than to submit to each other and address concerns face to face in private or in church courts—doing everything "decently and in order" (1 Cor 14:40). Our soul is too noble, our insight too keen, and our vision too soaring to be confined within the boundaries of a communion. Some will not bend their opinions to the common consent of the church; others will not limit what they think everyone should believe to that common confession. Some abandon the church altogether, while others make their own little corner in it for a private club.

When we leave the great sea of Christian communion to colonize our own rivers and shorelines, the party we lead becomes captive to our own narrow interpretations, views, and plans. Timothy was accountable to a council of elders to help keep him on track. Yet accountability is something that people, especially in my generation and younger, find difficult to accept in concrete terms.

Jesus did not establish a movement, a tribe, or a school, but a church. Whether our divisive ambition is determined by extraordinary ministers, scholars, or movements, it is completely out of step with "the pattern of the sound words" that is held humbly and guarded as a "good deposit" (see 2 Tim 1:13–14) that we all embrace because it is taught explicitly by the prophets and apostles as the ambassadors of Jesus Christ.

Reining In versus Reigning *In* Ambition

Ministers are not kings but servants. They die or move on, and they are replaced by someone else called to carry on the baton. It's about the ministry, not the minister. If unfaithful to their vows, they undergo a private trial of fellow pastors and elders. They may appeal the judgment to a broader assembly, but finally they have to submit to God's will expressed through the church. In other words, it is Christ's church, not ours. He wrote the constitution and he rules by his Word and Spirit, through the pastors and elders he gave us as gifts.

The New Testament prescribes an order in which pastors and elders are equal and accountable to each other in local and broader assemblies. As we see in Paul's encouragement to Timothy, ordinary pastors are called and replaced through a process of discernment in the church. The minister comes and goes, but the ministry endures — determined by the authority of Scripture rather than by the effectiveness or ingenuity of those who bear the office.

Part of our problem is that we've been shaped by a culture that is losing any sense of respect for *office*, even in secular affairs. In the past, office was distinguished from persons. In spite of one's view of the polities or the personal character of the president, he would always be referred to as "President So-and-So" or at least "Mr. So-and-So." Yet on the left and the right today, that is no longer customary. Even in elementary school, teachers are often called by their given name — or by their last name.

In many churches, the title "Pastor" has dropped out of ordinary conversation. At first, this seemed motivated by a desire to take pastors off of their pedestal. Yet in fact, it has the opposite effect. When we called them "Pastor," we were acknowledging that the office mattered, even if we weren't inclined to seek him out as a golfing partner. He could come or go and the ministry would go on, because it is not his ministry but Christ's.

But now there is tremendous pressure placed on pastors to be *persons* we like. We go to a particular church because we really connect with Jim. We tell people that we go to "Jim's church." We love Jim's ministry as if it were his personal base of influence rather than Christ's ministry that he shares with every other pastor. He's the kind of guy I could hang out with. Of course, I might soon discover that I can't actually hang out with Jim. I may never even see him at my house, making a visit to check on how my family and I are growing in Christ. In some cases, the sheep have never even met their shepherd. His person is so great that he cannot carry out his office. Then, if he falls, my faith may be shattered.

Compare this with the words of one of the Reformed confessions. Because "the preaching of the Word of God is the Word of God ... the Word itself which is preached is to be regarded, not the minister that preaches; for even if he be evil and a sinner, nevertheless the Word of God remains still true and good."[67] Of course, the person of the preacher matters. An evil pastor is, well, an evil pastor and should be removed. Nevertheless, he doesn't speak to us in his person but in his office. If it were to turn out that he never believed a word of it himself, his preaching of the Word, the baptisms he performed, and the Supper he regularly dispensed remain valid. They never were his personal words or sacramental actions, but Christ's.

Pastors may have some wonderful things to say, some interesting cultural insights, and some personal stories to make us feel connected to them. But in their office they are no longer private persons but Christ's ambassadors. Through this office assigned to them, God himself judges, justifies, and commands. Similarly, elders rule and deacons serve on Christ's behalf—not in their persons, but in assembly as office bearers.

Only Christ Has a Legacy

Timothy was to preach the Word and administer the sacraments to the same people he guided personally along with the elders. Paul never encouraged Timothy to contemplate his personal "legacy." There were no instructions about a succession plan. After all, he would be succeeded by those who, like him, were trained, tested, and ordained by the church's officers in assembly and most likely not selected single-handedly by Timothy.

It may come at first as a rebuke for us, especially as pastors, to hear that we have no legacy. It is Christ's legacy that he put into effect by his death (Matt 26:28; Heb 9:16–18) and dispenses from heaven by his Word and Spirit (Eph 4:7–13). In fact, in Ephesians 4 the pastors and teachers are "Christ's gift" (4:7). It is the Father's inheritance, won by Christ on behalf of his coheirs. We come and go, but the legacy keeps on being dispersed. The rebuke turns to comfort as we realize that it is Christ's church, that he is building it, and that we have the privilege simply of passing out the gifts for a while.

One example of the tendency to shift our focus from the ministry to the ministers, I believe, is the proliferation of multi-site churches. I am not in any way suggesting that those who favor a multi-site model of ministry are guilty of reckless ambition. I take it for granted that they are motivated by mission and would agree heartily with much else that I've argued here. My concern, however, is that the *model* is more susceptible to a greater focus on the minister than on the ministry.

Proponents define the multi-site church as "one church meeting in multiple locations." "A multi-site church shares a common vision, budget, leadership, and board."[68] Generally speaking, from a central location the main preaching/teaching pastor delivers a message that is then broadcast by video link-up to other sites. At these other sites there may be local fellowship, but most ministry decisions are made, so to speak, "at the top." Clearly, the ministry is concentrated ultimately in the movement's main founder and leader.

Such a pattern runs against the grain of the incarnation. It is not virtual presence but a real presence that Christ gives us when he speaks and acts among us. He did not remain in heaven while writing messages in the sky or on giant screens. He sent prophets in his name. Then, in the fullness of time, he came down himself—assuming our flesh. "My sheep hear my voice, and *I know them*, and they follow me" (John 10:27, italics added). If the Good Shepherd knows us by name, shouldn't his undershepherds? The technologies we use are not indifferent. They say something about the message itself.

A second problem is "itinerancy." It means a state of traveling from place to place. One of the concerns in the Reformation was that church leaders—especially bishops and archbishops—were not expected to actually preach, teach, or oversee a local church with a body of elders. Rather, they presided over the cathedral, which encompassed all of the local churches. The Church of England retained bishops, but its reformers insisted that bishops actually exercise their ministry in person at a local parish. This didn't mean that pastors could not exchange pulpits on occasion or speak at conferences, but it did mean that their calling as a minister depended on a specific call to a local church.

What is interesting is that the greatest degree of independence of bishops or ministers from the local church arose not in Roman Catholic or High Church traditions, but in evangelicalism. With the Great Awakening in Britain and America, ministers could work freely and unimpaired outside the "system" of mutual submission. John Wesley famously declared in his *Journal* (May 28, 1739), "The world is my parish."

Perhaps this is the best time to put my cards on the table. I do not expect everyone to agree with my presbyterian convictions, but I offer them for consideration because I am convinced that they are biblical. To state the position briefly, this system of government is neither hierarchical nor democratic but covenantal (federal or representative). Clearly, Scripture teaches that besides ministers who preach there are elders who rule and deacons who serve (Exod 24:9; Acts 14:23; 1 Tim 5:17; Titus 1:5; Jas 5:14; 1 Pet 5:1; Rev 4:4). Elder-led government is clearly attested by the apostles, along with qualifications for holding this office (1 Tim 3:1–13). Pastors and elders are "worthy of double honor," though for that reason, "Do not be hasty in the laying on of hands" (1 Tim 5:17, 22). So important was this to Paul that he could remind Titus, "This is why I left you in Crete, so that you might put what remained into order, and appoint elders in every town as I directed you" (Titus 1:5); this was followed by a list of their qualifications (1:6–9).

Whereas the apostles were called immediately and directly by Jesus in person and the whole world was indeed their parish, ordinary pastors are tested, ordained, and called to particular churches by the presbytery. It is striking that when Paul defends his office, he emphasizes the point that he did not receive it from the church or any of its leaders, but from Christ himself. Yet he reminds Timothy to take confidence in the gift he was given when the presbytery laid hands on him (1 Tim 4:14).

Thus, there are no apostles today, but ordinary pastors who

shepherd particular churches together with the elders. Pastors cannot rule independently from the body of elders. Therefore, the ruling body in a local church consists not of clergy but of laypeople.

At the Council of Jerusalem (Acts 15), representative elders were sent from the various churches to decide the matter of Gentile inclusion. Repeatedly the delegates are referred to as "the apostles and the elders." So even in the days of the apostles, authority was shared with the elders. Yet we read that "the whole church" came to agreement, through these representatives sent by each church. James and Peter spoke, but "the apostles and the elders" arrived at their decision by common consent. Peter was never singled out as possessing unique authority. Yet once the consensus was reached, it was a decision binding on all the churches. "Then it seemed good to the apostles and the elders, with the whole church, to choose men from among them and send them to Antioch with Paul and Barnabas" (15:22). Wherever they went, "they delivered the letter" to the churches (15:30). "As they went on their way through the cities, they delivered to them for observance the decisions [*dogmata*] that had been reached by the apostles and elders who were in Jerusalem. So the churches were strengthened in the faith, and they increased in numbers daily" (Acts 16:4–5).

Therefore, each local church was considered "the church," but only as it was in communion with the other churches. Pastors and elders met for mutual admonition and encouragement as well as to make decisions on behalf of the churches they represented. Cases could even be appealed to these broader assemblies, all the way to a general synod such as the one in Jerusalem. The ancient fathers confirm that this common consent of pastors and elders, in local and broader assemblies, had been the apostolic form of church government

As Jerome observed in the fifth century, the early churches were governed by pastors and elders together; it was only when ungodly ambition arose in the church that pastors jockeyed for greater positions of authority. Even this church father in Rome pointed out that "bishop" and "elder" were interchangeable terms.[69] Eventually, however, moderators of the presbytery became bishops and later one bishop—the bishop of Rome—claimed primacy. The Christian East as well as the later Reformers saw this as nothing less than an act of schism.

As noted above, advocates define a multi-site church as "one church meeting in multiple locations," sharing "a common vision, budget, leadership, and board."[70] Yet what they do not share are local pastors and elders. Even if some install elders in each location, the pastor is the gifted teacher whom they know only by his weekly appearance on the screen. Regardless of intentions, the medium ensures that he can never be the pastor, but only a celebrity teacher. By being the "pastor" of many churches, he is actually the pastor of none. Furthermore, it is *his* board that has the last word. This model seems far more hierarchical than the others it rebelled against. It also seems more likely to foster the temptation that all of us have toward ambition more than service, despite the best motives. Christ's global garden grows concretely only in local plots.

In all sorts of ways (by no means limited to the multi-site approach), churches today often reflect the influence of business models, with the pastor as the CEO or chairman of the board. Some large churches have been faithful from generation to generation because they have been intentional about appointing enough elders to oversee smaller groups. I have also seen plenty of small churches that are ingrown and do not foster outreach and fellowship.

Yet the pressures on the pastor—as well as elders and deacons—can be great. With the multiplication of ministers on staff, it is easier to gravitate toward a more hierarchical business model. And it is less likely that the sheep will come into physical contact with their shepherd when they are consumers of a service that a CEO oversees.

"Fear Not, Little Flock"

I think that if Jesus were to return today, he might tell us to stop taking ourselves so seriously. "*I* will build *my* church and the gates of hell shall not prevail against it" (Matt 16:18, italics added). The gates of hell are no small matter, at least for us. We're quite anxious. We have to do something about this (*this* being whatever we're shocked by at present). America is in moral free-fall. The media are persecuting us. Churches seem to be losing their way. Radical Islam is on the march—not to mention the perfect storm of AIDS, famine, and war that has taken millions of lives in Africa. Every time we turn on the news, our compassion or anger is aroused—to the point that we become numb to it. And people in the pews are numb to it, especially when the church places still more burdens on their shoulders.

This burden of extraordinary impact weighs heavily, first, on the shoulders of pastors. But here is the good news: it is not your ministry, church, or people. You do not have to create and protect a personal legacy, but simply to distribute and guard Christ's legacy entrusted to his apostles. You don't have to bind Satan and storm the gates of hell. Christ has already done this. We're just sweeping in behind him to unlock the prison doors. You don't have to live the gospel, be the gospel, do the gospel, and lead the troops to redeem culture and reconcile the world to God. We are not building a kingdom that can be convulsed with violence like other realms, but we are "*receiving* a kingdom that cannot be shaken" (Heb 12:28, italics added).

The disciples surely had reason to worry about the world's opposition. It was a little flock, and their King did not allow them to carry weapons. However, Jesus simply said to them and says now to us, "Fear not, little flock, for it is your Father's good pleasure to give you the kingdom" (Luke 12:32).

They had less trouble believing that they were a "little flock" than do we. We're still fairly invested in the vanishing legacy of Christendom. Many among us can remember when the church had considerable cultural and political clout. Now our solemn political pronouncements and moral sentiments are largely ignored. Yet once we are really convinced that Jesus Christ has already secured the victory of Satan, death, and hell, we can take a deep breath and be the "little flock" that he has already redeemed, doing what he has called us to do. It is marvelously liberating no longer to imagine that we have to build or preserve a kingdom that Christ was not building in the first place.

Thus, the reason for taking seriously the New Testament

principles of church order is not to create a formal hierarchy, but to guard against informal ones. "For what we proclaim is not ourselves, but Jesus Christ as Lord, with ourselves as your servants for Jesus' sake" (2 Cor 4:5). If Paul the apostle could say this, then surely ordinary ministers cannot claim any more for themselves. The treasure is the gospel ministry, not the minister. The weakness of it all is essential to keeping our focus where it belongs. "But we have this treasure in jars of clay, to show that the surpassing power belongs to God and not to us" (2 Cor 4:7).

Exercise

1. How do we idolize our leaders today — in the wider culture, but especially in the church? Is there a tendency to raise them too high in our estimation and then to tear them down when they fail to satisfy our own ambitions?
2. How does Scripture call us to rein in ambition, both as leaders and followers?
3. We hear a lot in churches today about the pastor's personal greatness, legacy, succession plans, and so forth. Do we put more emphasis today on ministers than on the ministry? If so, how?
4. What is the significance of Christ's assurance to his "little flock"? What does this mean for the way we often talk about our kingdom-building activities?

PART 2

ordinary and content

CHAPTER 7

contentment

The cure for selfish ambition and restless devotion to The Next Big Thing is contentment. But like happiness, excellence, and drive, contentment is not something you can just generate from within. It has to have an object. There must be someone or something that is so satisfying that we can sing, "Let goods and kindred go, this mortal life also."[71]

The gospel *is* truly radical: "the power of God for salvation" (Rom 1:16). Through this gospel, the Holy Spirit creates the faith to embrace Christ with all of his benefits. We are delivered from condemnation and are made part of the new creation in Christ. Filled with grateful hearts, we look for ways to glorify God and to love and serve our neighbors. We are eager to grow. Fueled by gratitude, we look for opportunities to glorify God and to love and serve others. Yet it is easy to take the gospel for granted. Then we find ourselves running out of that high-octane fuel, running out of gas in the middle of the busy highway of myriad calls to get in the fast lane. In the zeal created by the gospel itself, we can leave the gospel behind as we gravitate toward various calls to "something more."

Of course, there is something more to the Christian life than believing the gospel. The gospel keeps our eyes fixed on Christ, while the law tells us how to run the race. But our tendency is always to add our own doctrines to the gospel and our own commands and expectations to God's revealed Word. No longer content with the gospel and the commands of Scripture, we begin to look for *something more.* All the problems that I have described up to this point—and many others besides—result from a basic discontent with God's Word. We begin to look for programs and personalities that will make us winners in a sprint, instead of running the long-distance race with the assurance that Christ has already won the prize for us.

My thesis in this book is that we must turn from the frantic search for "something more" to "something more sustainable." We need to stop adding something more of ourselves to the gospel. We need to be content with the gospel as God's power for salvation. We also need to be content with his ordinary means of grace that, over time, yield a harvest of plenty for everyone to enjoy.

Sustainability

A relative newcomer, "sustainability" has entered our everyday language mainly from environmental science and economics. We've become increasingly aware that we can't just consume natural resources. At some point they run out or give out or are so changed by our manipulation that they become threats. The quarry becomes our grave. Even our attempts to save, recover, or build healthy ecosystems from scratch can yield unintended effects that are in the long run more damaging.

Applied to Christian discipleship, sustainable development is neither an oxymoron nor an impediment to progress. We should all be in favor of growth—both in numbers and in quality, in our personal lives and as churches. Where disagreements emerge is over what growth means and how it is sustained.

The danger of a mere conservationism is that it values "land" (the tradition) more than people who are now living on it and depend on it for their growth. At the other end of the spectrum are those who favor radical schemes that take little note of the spiritual ecosystem that has flourished for generations. Instead, according to this outlook, we need to focus on *this* generation and whatever it takes to create rapid growth. External forms are seen as restrictive. Churches and families can be viewed as hothouses where plants suffocate instead of replicating. So the solution is to get rid of the old vines and trellises. Start from scratch. You may have to lose a lot of people in the process, but that gives you a chance to start fresh without sheep slowing down the shepherds.

Or, to change the analogy, some will suggest that if you want to do something significant, you need to break away from the herd. Of course, in breaking away from one herd we inevitably join another. Instead of belonging to a local church — a flock determined by familiar routines that seem to make little measurable difference — we become part of the stampede of some new movement. Like most stampedes, we will tear up verdant pastures and gardens that have taken a long time to develop. Like "alternative music," we imagine that we're being countercultural and asserting our individual initiative when in fact we're still followers of the marketplace. Today's "radical" is tomorrow's "ordinary."

In most cases, impatience with the ordinary is at the root of our restlessness and rootlessness. We're looking for something more to charge our lives with interest, meaning, and purpose. Instead of growing like a tree, we want to grow like a forest fire.

Avarice: Ambition's Twin

In *The High Price of Materialism*, psychology professor Tim Kasser reveals data from his own empirical research into materialism and well-being. Consistent with other crucial studies that he cites, Kasser's conclusions are clear. Affluent cultures — and individuals — are not, on average, happier than others. In fact, although US income has doubled since 1957, the number of adults saying "that they are 'very happy' has declined from 35 to 29 percent."[72] Kasser observes:

> Social critics and psychologists have often suggested that consumer culture breeds a narcissistic personality by focusing individuals on the glorification of consumption (e.g., "Have it your way"; "Want it? Get it!"). Furthermore, narcissists' desire for external validation fits well with our conception of materialistic values as extrinsic and focused on others' praise.[73]

If ambition has been converted from a vice to a virtue, contentment has been transformed from a virtue into a vice. Think of how we use the word in normal conversations. It has come to mean settling for second best (which is always wrong). Lacking sufficient ambition, one is *content* to be something less than what he or she is capable of being.

Once again, something good has gone wrong here. We should not be content with stunted growth. We press on. And yet, we grow *from* a place of contentment — rest — and not *toward* it. I know, "more easily said than done." As on all the other points, I reiterate that I'm diagnosing an illness from which I suffer. We have to be constantly, patiently, and intentionally drawn out of the tragicomedy that we're writing for our life movie. We're turned outside-in and have to be turned inside-out — every day. This requires a lifetime of divine therapy: having our minds and hearts transformed by God's Word. We return to our baptism daily to find our true identity in Christ rather than in ourselves.

No longer turned outward to God in faith and to our neighbors in love, our fallen race has become, if not Icarus, then Narcissus. Disdaining those who tried to love him, the young man was fixated on his own beauty. One day, Nemesis lured Narcissus to a pond. Upon seeing his reflection, the tragic soul was trapped and he died in his own admiring gaze. The proper name for this is vanity, and it's as lethal as the myth intimates.

Something similar to ambition (the lust for praise) happened to avarice (the lust for wealth). Though hardly proto-socialists, the Protestant Reformers condemned the increasingly widespread view that money and property belonged ultimately to the people who made or inherited it. God gave wealth to people to hold and to use in public trust, to be put into circulation for the good of the commonwealth.

However, like its ambitious twin, avarice became a virtue in the early modern era. The "invisible hand" used to be God's providence, placing each of us in a vocation that serves the whole body. According to Adam Smith, however, it is the iron laws of the market that do this now. Each individual "intends his own gain," he argued, not thinking of directly contributing to the common good, while an "invisible hand" uses this self-interest for the greater good of all. In short, where self-interest reigns, all boats rise.[74] As with ambition, avarice is not yet a virtue but it has lost its vicious reputation. It can be channeled, harnessed, and directed to beneficial ends. Honesty begins its career as an objective virtue. Then it is justified on instrumental grounds (i.e., self-interest). And finally, when people realize that good guys don't always finish first, honesty becomes impractical. The transition from virtue to vice is complete. As Michael Douglas's character Gordon Gekko put it in the 1987 film *Wall Street*, "Greed is good."

Just as ambition can be adapted to a gospel of self-esteem, avarice can be "sanctified" as a prosperity gospel. These false gospels find their way into even more conservative churches that would be wary of full-strength versions.

Covenant, Not Contract

Beneath these full-strength or watered-down versions of narcissism is a *contractual* way of thinking. What do I mean by that? Take your marriage, for example. To view it as a contract is to treat your spouse as a service provider. You begin with the assumption that you're both sovereign individuals, free to choose whatever you want. You've both surrendered some of your freedom in exchange for certain benefits. As long as that works, great. If at some point your partner fails to keep his or her part of the bargain, you can get out of the contract. In the Age of Enlightenment, the idea of a social contract became the pattern for modern politics. Sovereign individuals cede some of their autonomy to the state in exchange for goods and services.

A *covenantal* way of thinking is different. In the biblical covenants, God is the sovereign Creator and Lord. We do not "own" ourselves, but we are God's image bearers, accountable to him not only for how we relate to him but also for how we relate to others. God speaks, and we hear. Therefore, we never start from a position of autonomy, electing to cede some of our sovereignty to God in exchange for certain benefits and securities. He gives us life, provides for us, commands us, and makes promises that he always fulfills according to his faithfulness. As his image bearers, then, we relate to each other covenantally: as husband and wife, as parents and children, and as members of the household of faith. In marriage, I yield my whole self to the other person and vice versa, regardless of poverty, sickness, or shortcomings, "till death us do part."

In a covenantal paradigm, I am bound intrinsically to God and to others in ways that transcend any good or service I can calculate. A total stranger rushes to the pond to pull out a young skater from the icy waters without running a cost-benefit analysis. The rescuer is not fulfilling a contractual obligation, but the command of God in his or her conscience that obligates a stranger to consider the endangered child a neighbor.

The contrast between contractual and covenantal maps of relationships can be seen implicitly in Tim Kasser's findings. He says that those who are driven by intrinsic values feel freer. They go to church because they want to, have close relationships because they desire the company of the other person, and so forth. Extrinsic values are expectations that one does not personally embrace but that one must at least pretend to exhibit in order to win approval or advancement. Theorists call this "contingent self-esteem," because it is always dependent on what others think, and "discrepancies" are specific ways in which one falls short of the standard of measurement.[75] "Thus, people with materialistic values hinge their self-esteem and self-worth on whether they have attained some reward (money) or whether other people praise them (say they look good, admire them, etc.)."[76]

It is not difficult to interpret these empirical findings from a biblical perspective. We crave approval, but we do not even know what the real measurement is even though we sense that we have fallen short of it. Suppressing our awareness of God, we shift the source of our validation to other people. Even many Christians today rarely ask, "Am I really measuring up to God's holy law?" Rather, they wonder whether they're measuring up to the expectations of other

Christians—or perhaps society at large. We mask our "discrepancies" (i.e., sins) with the rhetoric of being high achievers.

Materialism and narcissism go hand in hand, according to the studies, largely because of a sense of deep insecurity, anxiety, and need for approval.

> Thus it was not surprising to find that students with strong materialistic tendencies scored high on a standard measure of narcissism, agreeing with statements such as, "I am more capable than other people," "I like to start new fads and fashions," "I wish somebody would write my biography one day," and "I can make anybody believe anything I want them to."[77]

Materialism and narcissism are closely identified with the tendency to treat people like things, instruments of their own personal dreams.[78]

> Barry Schwartz has called these "instrumental friendships," writing that in capitalist, consumeristic societies all that is required is that each "friend" can provide something useful to the other. Instrumental friendships come very close to being market-like, contractual relations, with personal contact and the knowledge of mutual interdependence substituting for formal contractual documents.[79]

Christians in modern societies enter into scores of contracts, from credit cards to mortgages to employment. There's nothing sinful about contracts. The problem is that we allow a contractual (and consumeristic) thinking to expand into all areas of life. Our society trains us to think of marriage as a contract. If one has a lot of capital to protect, a prenuptial agreement might be added. And if one party fails to fulfill his or her end, the contract is null and void. Increasingly, children are raised in a contractual environment. Kasser quotes the president of the Intelligence Factory: "Parents always have to be managing their assets, including their children."[80]

When contractual thinking dominates our horizon of meaning, we can even make Jesus, the church, or our own spirituality an asset we think we can manage. On occasion, in the church of my youth, the pastor would give the invitation to come forward at the end of the service with the words, "Now you're signing a contract with God." You pray the prayer and then are told, "If you really meant that, you have a personal relationship with Jesus." Some of the evangelistic tracts even closed with a place to sign your name after the prayer. Jesus becomes my ultimate service provider if I choose him over the other offers. But when it doesn't seem to "work for me," we get out of the contract.

We even talk about "making Jesus my personal Lord and Savior," as if we could make him anything! This assumes that we start off as autonomous individuals who "own" ourselves in the first place. Then, if we choose, we can cede some of our sovereignty (or all of it perhaps) to Jesus, in exchange for whatever we think he can give us in return. The good news is that Jesus *is the only Lord and Savior*. It is not what we make him, but what he has made us—coheirs of his estate—that the gospel proclaims.

If our relationship with Jesus is like a contract, then we bring the same logic with us to church. We choose a local church the way we choose a neighborhood, a phone company, or a new car. We might become a member, or we might not. There may not even be membership (since that would be too formal and interfere with a person's relationship with Christ). Instead church leaders will bend over backwards to make sure people (at least the right people) are happy, because they know that you can go to the church down the highway, one that has a wider menu of options. With such anonymity, there is of course no church discipline—that is, genuine spiritual oversight and care. It's all part of the contract. If you are not fully satisfied with the service, there are plenty of other providers out there to make you happy at least for the time being.

Scripture reveals not only an original covenant of law with humanity in Adam, but a covenant of grace after the fall (Gen 3:15). Cain's line glimmers with the ambitious founders of culture, while Seth's is distinguished by the remark, "At that time people began to call upon the name of the LORD" (Gen 4:26). They acknowledged Yahweh not only as the covenant Lord who owned them by right of creation (signified by a tithe of the produce from their labors), but by the right of redemption (signified by animal sacrifice).

In the fullness of time, our promised Redeemer arrived. As the last Adam, Jesus is the covenant Servant who fulfilled all obedience that we owed. Yet as God, he is also the covenant Lord. So he is the Lord who commands and the human servant of the covenant who obeys. We know that the work he accomplished on our behalf has perfectly secured our reconciliation to and acceptance by God because he is the Lord who commands and the Servant who obeyed. "You did not choose me," Jesus tells us, "but I chose you" (John 15:16). Now, united to him through faith, we are counted just and are being conformed to his image. And we are also united to others "from every tribe and language and people and nation" (Rev 5:9), who have also been grafted into this vine. Our identity is no longer something we strive toward, based on an ambiguous standard and dependent on the approval of others. "Who shall bring any charge against God's elect? It is God who justifies" (Rom 8:33).

If that is true, I no longer have any reason to treat others as tools of my self-esteem and self-validation. I can finally accept the verdict that I have failed the test, because there is a perfect righteousness that has been imputed to me through faith in Christ. I am who I am ultimately not because of my choices, but because God chose me and these other justified and renewed sinners in addition to me. We simply rest in this security.

Now I can embrace these other people as gifts, knowing that together we are being refashioned according to the image of Christ. My brothers and sisters are not instruments of my ambition, but gifts—coheirs of the inheritance that we all share together in Christ. Yes, they're also needy, as I am. But God has given them gifts I need, and he has given me gifts they need. The smallest person in the eyes of the world may be the one God intends to pass along some fruit of paradise. Only God's saving grace can create this kind of covenantal community.

I can even embrace my non-Christian neighbors as those who, for all I know, are chosen from all eternity and redeemed, and will be united to Christ through my witness and that of other Christians. But working out its implications and living consistently with the word God has spoken is a lot of work. It involves perpetual warfare with our indwelling sin that feeds on the remnants of a story that we no longer confess to be true.

In the kingdoms of this age, contracts are still essential. Yet even when we enter into them, we know that there is something more basic to our humanity than such thin bonds can satisfy. I'm not simply an employer or employee, a provider or a consumer, a landlord or a renter; more basically I am a fellow image bearer of God even with those who are hostile to their Maker.

Imagine the difference that a covenantal way of thinking could make in our view of church membership, in our marriage and family life, and in our relationships with others at work and in the neighborhood. When everything turns on my free will, relationships—even with God—are contracts that we make and break. When everything turns on God's free grace, relationships—even with each other—become gifts and responsibilities that we accept as God's choice and will for our good and his glory.

In a certain sense, you didn't even choose your spouse. Sure, you may have chosen between one candidate and another, but the people we are and the people we marry change—for better and for worse—after the honeymoon. "That's not what I signed up for," we feel when the going gets rough. "She's not fulfilling her side of the bargain." "He's not providing what I thought he would—and what he did at first." These expressions betray a contractual way of thinking that fuels materialistic and narcissistic behaviors.

From our sharing in the fellowship of the Trinity, we can face the more contingent relationships that we encounter even in the church and our families—and certainly in our worldly callings. But we are going to have to suffer. Ironically, our ultimate desire—corrupted by sin—can only be finally attained through constant threats to many of our "felt needs," which are often shaped by pride, ambition, and avarice. By denying this ultimate desire in the interest of immediate gratification, we lose everything in the bargain.

So it is not simply by understanding doctrine that we uproot narcissism and materialism. It is by actually taking our place in a local expression of that concrete economy of grace instituted by God in Christ and sustained by his Word and Spirit. At least in its design, this economy is governed by a covenantal rather than contractual logic. In the covenant of grace, God says to us, "I'm with you to the end, come what may." Only from this position of security can we say the same to our spouse, children, and fellow believers. And from this deepest contentment we can fulfill our covenants in the world "as unto the Lord," even when others break their contracts.

Content with Our Father

So what does it mean to be content with God's provision? It means that when you and I are safely hidden with Christ in God through faith in his gospel, we are opened up to the others around us — first fellow saints, and then our other neighbors. Instead of being threats, they are fellow guests of God at his table. No longer competitors for commodities in a world of scarce resources, they are cosharers with us in the circulation of gifts that flows outward from its source without running out. After all, that source is the triune God: from the Father, in the Son, by the Spirit.

First, we find contentment in our King. "The earth is the LORD's and the fullness thereof" (Ps 24:1). We are not self-made, and ultimately we do not own anything. God owns all and he gives as it pleases him. We become content with our King as we grow in our understanding of who he is and what he has done. Our King is also our Father, who has adopted us as coheirs because we are united to his only Son. He is not a stingy monarch, and his generous gift-giving never depletes his storehouse (Matt 6:31 – 33; 11:28; Luke 11:9 – 13). So we do not need to jockey for his favor or for his gifts. Especially when we recall Golgotha, we never have to question whether he is disposed toward our good. We begin to rest in him and confide in him during life's storms when we know that he has chosen us, redeemed us, justified us, and adopted us, and that he is sanctifying us by his Spirit until we are one day glorified in Christ at his return.

God doesn't just command us, but he gives us a reason to be content. How do we know that God works everything together for his glory and our good?

> And those whom he predestined he also called, and those whom he called he also justified, and those whom he justified he also glorified.
>
> What then shall we say to these things? If God is for us, who can be against us? He who did not spare his own Son but gave him up for us all, how will he not also with him graciously give us all things? Who shall bring any charge against God's elect? It is God who justifies. Who is to condemn? Christ Jesus is the one who died — more than that, who was raised — who is at the right hand of God, who indeed is interceding for us. Who shall separate us from the love of Christ? Shall tribulation or distress, or persecution, or famine, or nakedness, or danger, or sword? ... No, in all these things we are more than conquerors through him who loved us." (Rom 8:30–37)

We are his not because of a victory we have achieved, but because of "the love of God in Christ Jesus our Lord" (8:39).

The writer to the Hebrews uses this sort of argument for our daily contentment: "Keep your life free from love of money, and be content with what you have, for he has said, 'I will never leave you nor forsake you.' So we can confidently say, 'The Lord is my helper; I will not fear; what can man do to me?'" (Heb 13:5–6).

Like Dracula, other lords have to gain their strength at the expense of others. Or even in just wars, rulers send others into a battle that they have declared. Only this King has walked alone and unarmed into the night to be willingly handed over to Satan, death, and hell in order to disarm the powers of darkness. Alone, he faced the wrath of justice, spilling his own blood not for loyal subjects but for enemies, winning their redemption and release by his glorious resurrection.

Content with Christ and His Kingdom

God is a strange economist, at least by our standards. First, he established in creation an economy of mutual gift exchange. The man does not dominate the woman, or vice versa. Each is created for the other, not as a tool in the will to power, but as a gift in the circulation of loving and serving relationships. Second, he created something even beyond this natural web of interdependence in the body of Christ, the church. It is not simply a natural covenant of human interdependence, but a covenant of grace, where we forgive as God has first forgiven us.

Christ's kingdom *is* extraordinary. We see this especially in Matthew 5–7, with the Beatitudes and the rest of the Sermon on the Mount. Christ's kingdom is extraordinary in its benefits. No longer inheriting a plot of land in the Middle East, with the threat of exile for disobedience hanging over our heads, we inherit the earth by grace alone. It is also extraordinary in the way of life that it creates.

Under the old covenant, strict justice was the standard. The kingdom of God was geopolitical. The land was holy and therefore God's enemies were to be driven out by holy war. Yet now Jesus calls us to love our enemies and to pray for our persecutors, who seek to drive us out of the common land that we share in this passing age. We are called not only to refrain from murder but also from hatred and retaliation—and, positively, to go over and beyond the call of duty in protecting the lives of others. Not only the physical act, but even lust, constitutes adultery. We are to live sacrificially, not demanding our due in court.

Where Christ is now the ultimate locus of identity, our true intimates are no longer the nuclear family, but the family of God. Jesus was preparing his followers for division: father against son, mother against daughter, brothers and sisters turning each other in to the authorities over conversion to Christ. The church is a city set on a hill, displaying in a small way what God has in store for humanity in the age to come. Even though the means that God uses are ordinary, the city that he is building isn't like anything this world has ever seen.

It is still an era of earthly citizenship and Caesars to whom we owe temporal obedience and respect. There are still courts. We still participate in common life. We still have families, whether we are married or single. In fact, for many of us they are covenant families where Christ unites rather than divides. But in the body of Christ a different economy is at work. Here, contracts are not operative — or at least they do not have the final word. It is the economy of the covenant of grace. Paul tells Timothy:

> But godliness with contentment is great gain, for we brought nothing into the world, and we cannot take anything out of the world. But if we have food and clothing, with these we will be content. But those who desire to be rich fall into temptation, into a snare, into many senseless and harmful desires that plunge people into ruin and destruction. For the love of money is a root of all kinds of evils. It is through this craving that some have wandered away from the faith and pierced themselves with many pangs.
>
> But as for you, O man of God, flee these things. Pursue righteousness, godliness, faith, love, steadfastness, gentleness. Fight the good fight of the faith. Take hold of the eternal life to which you were called and about which you made the good confession in the presence of many witnesses. (1 Tim 6:6–12)

The wealthy are not called to become poor, any more than the poor are encouraged to become rich. Rather, the wealthy are warned not

> to set their hopes on the uncertainty of riches, but on God, who richly provides us with everything to enjoy. They are to do good, to be rich in good works, to be generous and ready to share, thus storing up treasure for themselves as a good foundation for the future, so that they may take hold of that which is truly life.
>
> O Timothy, guard the deposit entrusted to you. Avoid the irreverent babble and contradictions of what is falsely called "knowledge," for by professing it some have swerved from the faith. (1 Tim 6:17–21)

No longer a star in my own movie, I can take my place in this gift exchange. The gifts that I have are not only for my private use, but for me to pass along to others. And the weaknesses I have are important because they make me more dependent on others. Although he repeatedly pleaded with God to take it away, Paul could even come to see his "thorn ... in the flesh" (whatever it was) as a gift of God, "to keep me from becoming conceited because of the surpassing greatness of the revelations" (2 Cor 12:7).

All of this means that the call to contentment is a summons to realize and accept our place in Christ and his body—and, more broadly, our place in the gift exchange in society through common grace. This cuts off at the root the discontentment—ambition—to change our station in life not only in the direction of prosperity, but also in a self-imposed poverty. "I know how to be brought low," Paul says, "and I know how to abound. In any and every circumstance, I have learned the secret of facing plenty and hunger, abundance and need. I can do all things through him who strengthens me" (Phil 4:12–13).

Restless pursuit of wealth or poverty is selfish ambition: the desire to rise above your peers and therefore out of that place in the circulatory system where God has placed you. Contentment is actually easier for those who leave the comforts of hearth and home to serve the disadvantaged in Africa than it is for those who live near the mall. If God has given you temporal wealth and position, use it for his glory and your neighbor's good.

Paul continues in Philippians, noting that he does not want to be a burden to anyone. "Yet it was kind of you to share my trouble." After noting their generous assistance, he says, "Not that I seek the gift, but I seek the fruit that increases to your credit." In other words, the healthy not only need the weaker members, but vice versa. Paul's weakness and physical need have played an important role in keeping the circulation going. "I have received full payment, and more.... And my God will supply every need of yours according to his riches in glory in Christ Jesus. To our God and Father be glory forever and ever. Amen" (Phil 4:14–20).

Content with His Ordinary Means of Working in Creation and Providence

"Expect a miracle!" That's good counsel if there is a promise in Scripture to back it up. The problem today is that many Christians are not looking for God's miraculous activity where he has promised it, namely, through his ordinary means of grace. Through these means, he has pledged to raise us from spiritual death, to forgive sins, to assure us of God's favor, and to conform us to Christ's image.

We believe in a big God who created the cosmos, became incarnate in the world, and secured redemption of this world by his life, death, and resurrection. We stand in awe of his mighty deeds in the past and the present and long for a glorious destiny that, to date, "no eye has seen, nor ear has heard" (1 Cor 2:9). But what if our addiction to superlatives has at least as much to do with cultural factors—factors that make it difficult to live with the ordinary?

If you're wondering whether your life counts if it consists of so many ordinary things every day, you are in good company. After all, God works through ordinary means every day in so many ways that we don't even notice his involvement and our complete dependence on him in each and every moment.

Typically, we identify "acts of God" with the big stuff: earthquakes, hurricanes, and parting seas. Or perhaps a better way of putting it: we identify the big stuff with what can be measured and recognized as an obvious miraculous intervention by God. Millions of people around the world will turn out for a prosperity evangelist's promise of signs and wonders. But how many of us think that God's greatest signs and wonders are being done every week through the ordinary means of preaching, baptism, and the Lord's Supper? If we associate God's activity exclusively with things that we can see and quantify—that is, his direct hand in the world—then we can fall unwittingly into the naturalist's habit of missing God's activity through normal people and things that he has made.

God uses means. Natural laws and human ingenuity are his tools, even when we do not see his hand. He didn't just establish these laws and then step away. As contemporary science reminds us, apparent chaos is ubiquitous. Things should fall apart, but they don't. Not for one moment could the cosmos sustain itself apart from the Father's loving word, which he speaks in his Son and by his Spirit.

Already in creation, God used means. Of course, the initial creation of the cosmos was a direct and immediate effect of God's command. We are told in Genesis 1 that God created matter ex nihilo — that is, out of nothing, in an instant. Yet regardless of how one interprets the "days," it is clear enough that the forming of our world did not happen all at once. It is easy to think otherwise when we focus exclusively on the initial command, "Let there be light" (Gen 1:3). However, we must see what goes before and after it. Before verse 3, the Spirit appears, "hovering over the face of the waters" (1:2). He is not simply a tourist, taking in the sights. Rather, he is preparing to perform that work that is unique to his person. In everything that the Trinity does, the Father is the source, the Son is the mediator, and the Spirit is the one who is at work within creation to bring the project to completion.

After verse 3, we see precisely why the Spirit's role is so important. The Father's speech now begins to separate and order the creation into its properly assigned realms, like a general dividing an army into regiments. The Father summons the separation of waters from waters (over which the Spirit was hovering) in verses 6–8, and then calls for the waters to be separated from dry land (1:9–10). God is now making the earth a place *to be inhabited*. Then we meet a string of commands that differ from the initial utterance, "'Let there be light,' and there was light." We read, "And God said, '*Let the earth sprout* vegetation, plants yielding seed, and fruit trees bearing fruit in which is their seed, each according to its kind, on the earth.' And it was so." All at once was it so? Not this time: "*The earth brought forth* vegetation.... And God saw that it was good" (1:11–13, italics added).

Not only was it a process; it was a natural process. But we have to get out of the habit of thinking that "natural" cancels divine activity. Natural processes are neither the ultimate cause nor useless. Now the earth is "bringing forth," bearing fruit. God is not creating each fruit, or even each tree, ex nihilo. Rather, now each tree and each piece of fruit bears within itself the seed needed to propagate itself. Yet God is commanding this process, surveying it, and pronouncing it good. It is still his word that is the source, but now it is a sustaining rather than originating word. And the Spirit is the one who works within creation to bring about its fruit-bearing response to the Father's summons.

This formula is repeated: "And God said, '*Let the waters swarm with swarms of living creatures....*' And God blessed them, saying, 'Be fruitful and multiply and fill the waters in the seas and let the birds multiply on the earth'" (Gen 1:20–22, italics added). "And God said, '*Let the earth bring forth* living creatures according to their kinds—livestock and creeping things and beasts of the earth according to their kinds'" (1:24, italics added). There's nothing to suggest that this was anything other than a normal and natural process. But does that make it any less the result of God's sovereign word?

What's true in creation is also true in providence. The birth of a baby doesn't have to be elevated to the status of a miracle to be an astonishing example of the wonder of God's ordinary way of working in our lives and in the world. We can't rule out miracles, but we also can't expect them. Miracles surprise us. But have we lost our joy in God's providential care, working through normal processes and layers of mediation that he himself has created and maintains by his Word and Spirit?

In every work of the Trinity, the Father speaks in the Son and by his Spirit, who is at work within creation to bring about the intended effect of that word. But God uses means, often many layers of means. This is actually for our good. Since no one can see God's face and live, we need God to wear various masks as he condescends to love and care for us. We pray, "Give us this day our daily bread." We don't expect it to fall from heaven. Rather, we know that God will give it to us through farmers and bakers and warehouse employees and truck drivers and shop clerks, and so on.

Once we recover a greater sense of God's ordinary vocation as the site of his faithfulness, we will begin to appreciate our own calling to love and serve others in his name in everyday ways that make a real difference in people's lives.

God's ordinary way of working includes the vocations of non-Christians. The first time I read the following statement from the reformer John Calvin, I was taken aback:

If we regard the Spirit of God as the sole fountain of truth, we shall neither reject the truth itself, nor despise it wherever it shall appear, unless we wish to dishonor the Spirit of God. For by holding the gifts of the Spirit in such slight esteem, we condemn and reproach the Spirit himself.[81]

It made me think twice because, although it's hardly jarring to say that God gives good gifts to unbelievers (Ps 104:27 – 30; Matt 5:45; Acts 14:17; 17:26 – 27), I am used to associating the Spirit with his work within the hearts of his elect. Calvin here is affirming God's common grace, even among the ungodly. He is targeting radical Protestants who claimed that only Christians could rule and create a godly culture. He adds:

> Whenever we come upon these matters in secular writers, let that admirable light of truth shining in them teach us that the mind of man, though fallen and perverted from its wholeness, is nevertheless clothed and ornamented with God's excellent gifts.... What then? Shall we deny that the truth shone upon the ancient jurists who established civic order and discipline with such great equity? Shall we say that the philosophers were blind in their fine observation and artful description of nature? Shall we say that those men were devoid of understanding who conceived the art of disputation and taught us to speak reasonably? Shall we say that they are insane who developed medicine, devoting their labor to our benefit? What shall we say of all the mathematical sciences? Shall we consider them the ravings of madmen? No, we cannot read the writings of the ancients on these subjects without great admiration.... Those men whom Scripture calls "natural men" were, indeed, sharp and penetrating in their investigation of inferior things. Let us, accordingly, learn by their example how many gifts the Lord left to human nature even after it was despoiled of its true good.[82]

Even unbelievers can rule justly and prudently, as Paul writes about the more pagan circumstances of his day (Rom 13:1 – 7). In addition to these natural remnants, there is the concept of common grace in Calvin, "not such grace as to cleanse it [nature], but to restrain it inwardly." This grace is tied to providence, to restraint; "but he does not purge it within." Only the gospel can do this.[83]

In other words, the sphere of God's activity has widened to

include the Spirit as well as the Father and the Son, ordinary providence as well as extraordinary miracle, and natural means as well as direct actions. It also has widened to encompass God's work in common grace, among all people, as well as his saving grace toward the elect. And not only does this work of the Spirit in common grace make it possible for us to be a blessing to unbelievers; it also makes their vocations and labors a blessing to us as well. Blessings do not have to be holy and saving in order to come from God, who is the giver of all good gifts to everyone.

Content with His Ordinary Way of Working in Redemption

No greater instance of the Spirit's working through creaturely media may be found than in the incarnation of the Son. Not only is all of creation upheld "in him" (Col 1:16–17); his own life displays examples of God's ordinary providence. Like the ex nihilo fiat, "Let there be light," the miracle of the incarnation is the eternal Word's assumption of our humanity from the Virgin Mary. Like the old, the new creation can only emerge by the direct and immediate fiat-word of God. Echoing Genesis 1, the angel explains to Mary in Luke's gospel that "the Holy Spirit will come upon you," ensuring that the fruit of her womb is no less than the Son of God (Luke 1:34–35, 38).

The Spirit, who hovered over the waters, dividing and uniting and bringing the Father's word to completion, "will come upon" the waters in Mary's womb. He will bind the eternal Son to the human nature that he receives from Mary. The virgin replies, "Let it be to me according to your word," because the same Spirit who was at work in her womb is already at work in her heart to bring about her "Amen!" to the word. Wherever we encounter not only the Father's speech in the Son, but the Spirit's "bringing forth" of inspired speech from human witnesses, the new creation dawns. Both the incarnation and Mary's consent are won by the Spirit's speaking through his Word.

Of course, the eternal Son's incarnation was extraordinary. Like "'Let there be light,'" it was a direct miracle. So too were his signs and wonders culminating in his own resurrection. Nevertheless, his gestation and birth were a normal nine-month process as he assumed our humanity and not instantaneous creation, as in Genesis 1:11 – 12: "'Let the earth sprout vegetation.'. . . The earth brought forth vegetation." Nor was Jesus a child prodigy: "And the child grew and became strong, filled with wisdom. And the favor of God was upon him. . . . And Jesus increased in wisdom and in stature and in favor with God and man" (Luke 2:40, 52). "Although he was a son, he learned obedience through what he suffered" (Heb 5:8). He was not born outside of time or our human nature; rather, he was born "when the fullness of time had come" (Gal 4:4).

Imagine Jesus learning Mary's favorite psalms and asking Joseph questions in the shop about God and life while they were making chairs. Daily, ordinary, seemingly little stuff that turns out to be big after all. Even his crucifixion was just another Roman execution, as far as what the onlookers witnessed. And yet, through it, God was reconciling the world to himself.

Not only in his incarnation but in his life and ministry, Jesus was always dependent on the Spirit as he fulfilled his Father's word (Matt 12:28). In fact, attributing his miracles to the devil is something that Jesus calls "blasphemy against the Holy Spirit" (12:31 – 32; Luke 12:10). Even after spending three years at Jesus' side, the disciples' understanding of, much less testimony to, Christ's person and work depended on the descent of another witness from heaven: the Holy Spirit (Acts 2).

Then the same Spirit brings about within us the "Amen!" of faith to all that Christ has accomplished. The Spirit who hovered over the waters in creation and the waters of Mary's womb unites us to Christ through water and his Word. The Spirit who indwelt the temple and rested on Jesus now indwells us permanently, individually and collectively, as his end-time sanctuary in a sea of death. Because of this, we not only are made alive by the fiat command, "Let there be light," but we bear the fruit of the Spirit by his working in our hearts through his ordinary means.

Then think of the way the Father unites us to his Son by his Spirit today. "So faith comes from hearing, and hearing through the word of Christ" (Rom 10:17). A normal process: a fellow sinner is sent by God to proclaim the forgiveness of sins to me in Christ's name, and I believe and am thereby saved (10:14–15). Baptism seems less dynamic than, say, raising someone from the dead or giving sight to the blind. Yet we are "baptized for the forgiveness of sins" and we "receive the gift of the Holy Spirit" (Acts 2:38). What can the regular administration of the Lord's Supper accomplish, with the most ordinary daily bread and wine as the elements? Nothing by themselves, but through it God promises to deliver Christ with all of his benefits (1 Cor 10:15–17).

We keep looking for God in all the obvious places. Obvious, at least, to the natural eye. But God chooses to be present in saving blessing where he has promised, in the everyday means that are available to everyone and not just to the spiritual "storm trackers." We don't climb up into heaven or descend into the depths to find God. Christ is present where he has promised; that's the argument Paul makes in Romans 10.

If our God is so keen to work in and through the ordinary, maybe we should rethink the way we confine him to the theatrical spectacles, whether the pageantry of the Mass or the carefully staged healing crusade. It takes no honor away from God that he uses ordinary — even physical — means to bring about extraordinary results. On the contrary, it underscores the comprehensive breadth of his sovereignty over, in, and within creation as the Father, the Son, and the Holy Spirit.

To be content with Christ's kingdom is to be satisfied also with his ordinary means of grace. This is a big one. We have trouble believing that weak things like a fellow sinner speaking in Christ's name, both judgment and forgiveness, could actually expand Christ's kingdom throughout the earth. Sure, there are sermons. We need good teachers. But surely a growing church needs something more impressive that will catch people's attention than the regular proclamation of and instruction in God's Word. After all, it's not by preaching the gospel but by living it that we draw people to Christ. Surely, doing more in our community will make a larger impact than weekly prayers, especially for the mundane concerns that are common to everyone. At the very least, we need to have sermons that focus on topics that our neighbors might find more helpful or interesting. And yet, our King tells us that "faith comes from hearing and hearing through the word of Christ" (Rom 10:17). Through the lips of a fellow sinner, Christ judges, justifies, and renews us here and now. The verdict of the final judgment is actually rendered in the present through this speech.

It might not be a bad idea that we learn the faith through a catechism week after week, or that we follow a liturgy that makes the Word of Christ dwell in us richly. But it all becomes so routine. We need to break it up with powerful events with impressive staging. Or perhaps a new program. But Scripture repeatedly urges us to grow in the grace and knowledge of Christ by regular instruction in "the pattern of the sound words" (2 Tim 1:13).

Baptism has its place. We may not be sure what it means, but we know that Jesus commanded it. A big part of the problem here is that we think of baptism as our work—testifying to our faith and promise to follow the Lord—rather than God's testimony and promise-making to us that delivers Christ with all of his benefits. Could there not be a more dramatic way of entering Christ's kingdom and making radical disciples? Hear Colossians 2:12: "having been buried with him in baptism ... you were also raised with him through faith in the powerful working of God, who raised him from the dead." God's promise comes first, and then faith embraces it.

Then there is the Lord's Supper. We may not have it often (so it doesn't get old), but again, Jesus commanded it. Yet how could a morsel of bread and a sip of wine be more successful than spiritual disciplines or small groups in binding us to Christ and each other? Here too we think of the event more as an opportunity for us to do something—to recall Jesus' death and to stir us to rededicate our lives to him—than God's means of grace. If it's chiefly about our activity, surely we could do something together that would be more successful in making Christ present and relevant in our lives and in our world. Hear 1 Corinthians 10:16: "The cup of blessing that we bless, is it not a participation in the blood of Christ? The bread that we break, is it not a participation in the body of Christ?"

In Scripture, miracles — God's extraordinary works — cluster around fresh stages of redemptive history. They authenticate new stages of revelation. The miracles that he performed through our Lord as well as through the prophets and apostles are sufficient to establish the credibility of the new covenant that Jesus put into effect by his death. Above all, his resurrection is the climactic event that secures and signifies the dawn of the new creation. Of course, God can do as he wishes, and it is not wrong to pray for miracles. Yet we have no promise in Scripture that those prayers will be answered in the way that we had hoped. We do have God's promise that he will perform the greatest signs and wonders through the preaching of his Word and the administration of his sacraments.

Again, we are drawn to the theology of the cross over against theologies of glory. The former is content to receive God as he discloses himself, in humility, poverty, and weakness. God reveals himself by hiding himself. He comes to us incognito, as a King dressed like a pauper, in order to serve us.

The rapid growth of life-saving and life-enhancing medicine is not a sign of God's absence, but of his daily care. The antidote to a naturalism that attributes healing ultimately to doctors and medicine is not to "expect a miracle," but to thank God for the myriad ways in which he has provided for us through the work of his own hands. We should marvel at God's care, wisdom, and loving involvement in every detail of our lives.

Today, we have no further resurrections to certify the gospel, but we have the testimony of eyewitnesses — the apostles who gave their lives in martyrdom for their proclamation of Christ. We are delighted with miracles with which God might surprise us, but God's final stage in his plan of redemption is the marvelous return of Jesus on the clouds of heaven. Until then, we are given eyes of faith to recognize God's loving care through everyday people and occasions.

Just as we wouldn't have expected to find the Creator of the universe in a feeding trough of a barn in some obscure village, much less hanging, bloody, on a Roman cross, we do not expect to find him delivering his extraordinary gifts in such human places and in such humble ways as human speech, a bath, and a meal. This can't be right, we reason. We need signs and wonders to know that God is with us. Yet it is only because God has promised to meet us in the humble and ordinary places, to deliver his inheritance, that we are content to receive him in these ways. If the apostles themselves could only find God in the most unlikely of places, how can we imagine that we can find him naked in glory rather than meet him clothed with his gospel, coming in peace?

CNN will not be showing up at a church that is simply trusting God to do extraordinary things through his ordinary means of grace delivered by ordinary servants. But God will. Week after week. These means of grace and the ordinary fellowship of the saints that nurtures and guides us throughout our life may seem frail, but they are jars that carry a rich treasure: Christ with all of his saving benefits. Whatever gifts may spill over into other activities and venues, it is by sharing in the ordinary service of Christ to his people each week that we become heirs of eternal life and draw others into his everlasting kingdom. Christ is the host and the chef. It is his event. His ministers are simply waiters delivering to his guests some savory morsels of the Lamb's everlasting wedding feast.

The covenantal outlook I've described transfers us from a debt economy to a gift economy. It's not an abstract antithesis between activity and passivity, or between choosing and being chosen. It's not even that we have fewer choices to make in this outlook. The real difference is whether our choosing is ultimate, whether our choices determine our identity, or whether our identity (which God chose for us) determines our choices. Throughout John 15, Jesus also issues imperatives to bear fruit that witnesses to the life-giving vine and to our own sharing in Christ. Yet our decisions, choices, and actions are grounded in his. Now we are free to choose the one who has chosen us, free to bind ourselves to a local expression of his chosen people simply because it is the family he is creating by his Spirit through his Word and sacraments.

True contentment, therefore, comes first from resting in Christ. The world's options are just too limiting. There is nothing on its menu for "being chosen by God," "redeemed and reconciled to the Father in his Son," "the forgiveness of sins and justification of the wicked," "being crucified and raised with Christ as part of his new creation," "belonging to God's new family," and "the resurrection of the body unto life everlasting."

Whenever the apostle Paul speaks of contentment, he always grounds it in this gospel. At least in principle, and gradually in practice, ambition loses its motivation. It is out of an ultimate place of rest that we find the strength to work for others. Avarice loses its rationale, since the real world behind the narrow gate is already ours in Christ. Martin Luther put it well: "I have held many things in my hands, and have lost them all; but whatever I have placed in God's hands, that I still possess."[84]

God has already "blessed us in Christ with every spiritual blessing in the heavenly places, even as he chose us in him before the foundation of the world, that we should be holy and blameless before him" (Eph 1:3–4). "In him we have redemption through his blood, the forgiveness of our trespasses, according to the riches of his grace, which he lavished upon us" (1:7–8). He is the one who is gathering all things together into his Son, whether things on earth or in heaven (1:9–10), with the Holy Spirit as "the guarantee of our inheritance until we acquire possession of it, to the praise of his glory" (1:11–14).

Contentment is the virtue that contrasts with restlessness, ambition, avarice. It means realizing, once again, that we are not our own—as pastors or parishioners, parents or children, employers or employees. It is the Lord's to give and to take away. He is building his church. It is his ministry that is saving and building up his body. Even our common callings in the world are not really our own, but they are God's work of supplying others—including ourselves—with what the whole society needs. There is a lot of work to be done, but it is his work that he is doing through us in daily and mostly ordinary ways.

Exercise

1. What is the relevance of the idea of "sustainable development" for our growth in Christ?

2. What is "avarice" and how has it become increasingly virtuous in our culture? Can you think of concrete ways in which you feel this temptation in your own life?

3. Explore the difference between a "covenantal" and "contractual" outlook on life. Are there specific ways in which you feel drawn toward the latter? How do we challenge that way of thinking from a biblical perspective?

4. What are the biblical grounds for our contentment in life?

CHAPTER 8

we don't need another hero

I don't quite agree with the title of this chapter. I think we still need heroes. We need people for our sons and daughters—and ourselves—to look up to. My point here, though, is that the hero-thing has been overdone. It's not even faithful to Scripture, for reasons I will unpack below. And it tends to reduce Christ to the Ultimate Hero, when what he means to us and for us is so much greater than that.

For many of us reared in the church, the example of heroes is deeply woven into the curriculum of our earliest memories. In Sunday school, the Old Testament was a gold mine for Bible heroes. Abraham is the man of faith, willing even to sacrifice his son at God's command (aside from the fact that he kept questioning God's promise and even told a king that Sarah was his sister, to save his own skin). Moses—well, Moses is Moses: there are lots of heroic episodes to pick out from his life. (Just don't mention the part where God wanted to kill him because he was delaying circumcising his son, or the scene where he disobeyed God and was barred from entering Canaan.) David's virtues as "a man after God's own heart" are exhibited (while often skipping over his adultery and indirect murder, and the violence that kept God from letting him build the temple). Samson's strength is encouragement to manly opposition to the world, the flesh, and the devil. Prophets like Nathan, Elijah, and Elisha show us how to say no to idolatry, and so forth.

This does not mean that we aren't supposed to glean anything from the examples of these figures. But there are at least three reasons why we should be wary of making this the focus. First, the stories themselves don't glamorize. Coming back to them as adults, we're often struck with the fact that, like us, every single Bible hero acted unheroically, often falling into a cycle of sin or despair. We tend to turn the Bible's stories into something like *Aesop's Fables* or the saccharine "Christian novels" that make these biblical narratives far less interesting—and true to life—than they actually are. Even when such figures foreshadow Christ, they soon fall short and remind us why they need a Savior as much as the rest of us.

Second, we have to see how the New Testament interprets these stories. Yes, they're "examples for us," as Paul says, but in context (referring specifically to the unbelieving generation in the desert in 1 Corinthians 10), he says that they are examples to warn us against unbelief. Hebrews 11, often dubbed "The Hall of Heroes," is filled with people who—according to the original stories themselves—were not always heroic. The writer of Hebrews uses these examples to build the cumulative case that it was by faith—faith in Christ—that they held fast to God's promise and thereby overcame the world's assaults. The more sordid scenes of their biography were just as essential to highlight in order to focus on this very point.

We must read these episodes in the light of the whole plot of Scripture, which coalesces around Christ. And that's my third concern about reducing the Bible to a collection of "Dare to Be a Daniel" tales. Even the most heroically faithful figures in the Bible—at their best—fall short of the kind of Savior we need. It becomes clear from the story itself that they too need to be redeemed from the guilt and power of sin. We don't just need another hero. We need God to descend to earth and rescue us.

The saturation of "Bible hero" vignettes is often followed by a trail of other great men and women. After all, you soon run out of biblical examples. So we turn to the great people in Western history. Again, there is nothing wrong about inculcating virtue by learning about those who displayed it and by shunning the examples of those who were characterized by vice. Yet the constant drumbeat is exemplary figures.

In more conservative circles, we even try to recruit people like America's founders and other national heroes. It matters little that many of them were clearly skeptical of orthodox Christianity; they were moral theists, at least deists, and that's enough to serve as moral inspiration. But we hardly need churches to inculcate an appreciation for the justly celebrated accomplishments of these great figures. It points up how far we will go to adorn the gospel with Christian heroes, even if we have to fudge a bit on what constitutes Christianity itself.

Then later, perhaps in youth group, we're introduced to contemporary celebrity athletes and entertainers who "know the Lord." Again, their hectic schedule may make it impossible for them to belong to a church (or at least to attend regularly), but they express a deep and very personal "relationship with Jesus."

How many youth pastors bring in the elderly couple who has walked with the Lord through ups and downs, which exposes teenagers to their godly wisdom? What about the brother who never misses an opportunity to share the gospel with kids at the school that he cleans during the week as janitor? Or the sister who has struggled with doubts and despair through an ordeal with cancer, but who knows that in the next six months she's been given to live (according to doctors), her life is not her own but belongs to her faithful Savior Jesus Christ?

Years ago, the pastor typically taught the youth catechism, preparing them to profess their faith publicly as communicant members. The shift from catechism classes to Sunday school, and then to the youth group, tended to distance believers from the church at precisely the moment that they were supposed to take that next step of maturity. And why do we think that young people need to hang out with other young people, led by a guy who is only a little older? I'm not saying that we shouldn't have youth pastors. But I am questioning the factors that have gone into this transition from the apostolic model (older teaching younger, as in Titus 2:4) to one that is more culturally driven.

What do such transitions say about what we value? Where did we get the idea that older folks need to be given a "kid-free" environment with other "golden oldies," and that men's groups and women's groups are more meaningful than the communion of saints? For each of these markets the faith is packaged in a way that distinguishes their interests and needs from those of the rest of the body. There are study Bibles and programs for every conceivable demographic. Often the notes seem more aimed at making relevant applications than in helping people understand the Bible itself.

To the extent that most of our formation in church happens in these niche groups, what forms us will be less the common faith we share than the questions, concerns, and takeaways that we read into it. Again, I'm not against the free association of believers in social settings, but I am simply asking the question: Are we dividing what God has joined together? Is "community" for us more contractual than covenantal, determined more by social locations other than Jesus Christ?

Of course, we need people to look up to, especially in an age of acute ambition—which is another good reason to have older saints mentoring the younger. More than heroes, though, we need a Savior. Then we also need ordinary people around us who exemplify godly qualities and take the time to invest in our lives. Paul even called his young apprentices and churches to follow his example. Yet the characteristics he mentions are his undistracted focus on the gospel, humility, love for all the saints, and contentment (2 Thess 3:9).

Ordinary Callings: Cultural Transformation or Loving Service?

First, the call to radical transformation of society can easily distract faith's gaze from Christ and focus it on ourselves. Such people hold that the gospel has to be something more than the good news concerning Christ's victory. It has to expand to include our good works rather than to create the faith that bears the fruit of good works. The church has to be something more than the place where God humbles himself, serving sinners with his redeeming grace. It has to be the home base for our activism, more than being the site of God's activity from which we are sent and scattered like salt into the world.

There is a marked tendency in this emphasis to play off the "kingdom" against "church." After all, all of life is worship. We can't *go* to church, because we *are* the church, we are told by advocates of this approach. We aren't receiving a kingdom through Christ's Word and Spirit, but building it. Our good works are not the fruit of faith, which comes by hearing the gospel and is confirmed by the sacraments; rather, we are called to live the gospel, even to be the gospel.

Far too many people hold that it's not who we are that determines what we do, but what we do that determines who we are. Community service becomes something more than believers simply loving their neighbors through their ordinary callings in the world. It becomes part of the church's missionary task. It's not what we hear and receive, but what we are and do that gives us a sense of identity and purpose. We need something more than the gospel to trust in — or at least the gospel has to be something more than the life, death, and resurrection of Jesus Christ for sinners. Apparently, Jesus got the ball rolling, but we are his partners in redeeming the world.

Instead of following the example of John the Baptist, who pointed away from himself to "the Lamb of God, who takes away the sin of the world" (John 1:29), we offer our own lives and transformations as the good news. But this is to deny the gospel and therefore to cut off the power of true godliness and neighbor love at its root.

Second, radical views of cultural transformation actually harm our callings in the world. The most basic problem is that it reverses the direction of God's gift giving. According to Scripture, God gives us life, redeems us, justifies us, and renews us. He does this by his Spirit, through the gospel — not just in the beginning, but throughout our lives. Hearing this gospel, from Genesis to Revelation, is the means by which the Spirit creates faith in our hearts. United to Christ, our faith immediately begins to bear the fruit of evangelical repentance and good works. We offer these works not to God for reimbursement, but to our neighbors for their good. If we reverse this flow of gifts, nobody wins. God is offended by our presumption that we could add something more to the perfect salvation he has won for us in his Son. We are therefore on the losing side of the bargain, and our neighbors are too, since our works are directed to God on our behalf rather than to our neighbors on God's behalf.

Third, despite its affirmation of our callings in the world, the call to change the world undervalues ordinary vocations that actually keep God's gifts circulating. A carpenter, chef, or homemaker may know what it means to provide excellent service to others every day. In fact, they're more likely to know the standards of excellence in their own field better than their pastor. But what does it mean to be a "world changer"? What does it mean to redeem your workplace, somehow annexing the office, lab, or shop to the kingdom of Christ? It is not always clear what this would look like on the ground, but we're attracted to the vision of making a big impact—as quickly as possible. But like the others, this weighty expectation can turn rather quickly from enthusiasm to exhaustion. I'm not questioning whether Christ is Lord over all of life. Rather, the question is how he exercises his lordship in the various overlapping activities of our life. Does he require faithfulness or measurable impact in society attributable to direct Christian action?

Fourth, the call to radical transformation of society can feed a spiritualized version of upward mobility. If direct cultural impact is the goal, it's easy to adopt an elitism that places a premium on high-profile callings. We hear this on the left and the right in our circles. It's fine to be a homemaker, baker, or diving instructor. But what we really need are lawyers, politicians, artists, economists, scientists, *New York Times* editorialists, entertainers, and sports celebrities. These are "strategic" positions, it is often said. There aren't a lot of agendas available for redeeming janitorial services.

Fifth, the culture-transforming mission can backfire in the other direction, against those who are in fact called to be novelists, painters, physicists, senators, and academics. They too are called by God to ordinary labors in the common culture that they share with non-Christians. When we expect them to somehow advance Christ's kingdom as the elite guard in his culture war, the result is often disastrous. An economist knows the complexity of his or her field and how and why Christians with the same theological convictions can nevertheless differ markedly over theories and agendas. That is because Scripture does not give us an economic blueprint for nations in this time between Christ's two advents.

Consequently, God's common grace—enjoyed by believer and unbeliever alike—illumines people to study the relevant data and theories. It is precisely at this stage where Christians who agree over the same doctrine or principle will differ over the wisest strategy for applying it. The same is true of artists, who eschew simplistic and sentimental windows on the world; of politicians, who realize that public service is about compromise for the common good; of scientists, who marvel at fellow believers who reduce their discipline to ideology as much as secularists.

Reforming Our Theology of Culture

I suspect that our obsession of late with cultural transformation in evangelical circles facilitates the thinly "Christianized" versions of ambition, restless innovation, and impatience that actually make any real kind of culture, Christian or otherwise, impossible.

In the closing decades of the twentieth century, evangelicals suddenly became a cultural force in American society. Of course, there have always been socially-engaged voices in our circles, but nothing like this concerted level of engagement. It was a movement that determined the outcome of many elections. Yet now, in recent years, the predictable reaction has occurred—not only from society at large (which now has a fairly dim view of evangelicals), but within the movement as well.

On balance, this movement—known as the Christian Right—was a failure. I have neither the space nor the competence to offer a detailed account. However, I do have some supportable conclusions about some of the things that went wrong.

First, I think that the movement was shallow both theologically and culturally. Theologically, the movement to my mind displayed a shallow view of God, creation, the complex nature of sin, redemption, and the church especially in its relation to culture. Many of those who were given to apocalyptic predictions read the Bible in one hand with the newspaper in the other. Expectation of imminent destruction of "the late, great planet earth" merged with an ideal of changing the world, or at least America. It was a combustible mixture. In short, the theological coordinates were not well thought out as evangelicals stormed the gates.

A correspondingly shallow view of culture was also evident on many levels. While mainline Protestants are prone to follow the fads and fashions of high culture (the academy, arts, and sciences), evangelicals have usually been the patrons of popular culture. Thus, energy was focused on making a cultural splash through celebrity Christians and politics. This further reinforced the sense both that politics (specifically, government) is the main driver of culture and that evangelical churches formed another special-interest voting block. Not surprisingly, our neighbors' reaction to evangelicals rises and falls with the winds of political patronage.

Cheered by initial success in rallying the troops, the leaders of the Christian Right continually added to their list of demands. The laudable concern to protect human life from the ravages of abortion-on-demand spread quickly to a host of policy initiatives that reflected the Republican platform more than serious biblical exegesis. In the meantime, the evangelical left seemed captive to the Democratic Party. All of this stands in sharp contrast to Roman Catholic engagement, which was able to draw on centuries of social thought.

In short, I believe that the unrealistic call to cultural transformation is in large part to blame. Younger evangelicals may tone down the rhetoric and switch political allegiances in the ongoing culture war. They may be more culturally savvy than the previous generation. Yet the tie that remains is this: the illusion that we can make the kingdoms of this age the kingdom of Christ and that this is done chiefly through direct (especially political) action.

The alternative to the ideal of cultural transformation is not passivity. Much less does Scripture allow a separation of one's calling in Christ from one's callings in the world. We are not Christians at prayer and pagans at work. Our biblical convictions shape our approach to all questions of life. Yet that is precisely why we need to evaluate those convictions. We need to recover our biblical bearings. If we mature in our theological convictions and assumptions about the nature of culture, we will begin to see that societies, like churches, are shaped over long periods and through all of the various callings that occupy us every day.

We are living in the time between Christ's two advents: the "already" and the "not yet" of our salvation. Only when Christ returns will he directly judge the nations and reign over his restored cosmos in everlasting *shalom*: justice and peace. "For in this hope we were saved." But Paul goes on to add: "Now hope that is seen is not hope. For who hopes for what he sees? But if we hope for what we do not see, we wait for it with patience" (Rom 8:24–25). What we need, therefore, is a way of thinking about a relative justice and peace in a fallen world that lies under the dominion of sin and death.

We are citizens of God's new creation in Christ, but we are also citizens of the common kingdoms and cultures in which God's providence has placed us. God is building his kingdom in this world through his Word and sacraments, but we know that the kingdoms of this age will not be made the kingdom of Christ until his return. We live as salt and light, but with no illusions of Christendom. So we are neither utopian nor passive. Rather, Christ is building his church (Matt 16:18), and we are "receiving a kingdom" by God's grace in the body of Christ (Heb 12:28; cf. Luke 12:32). The redemption that Christ has already won objectively for us is not only the salvation of the soul, but the resurrection of the body; not only of people, but of a renewed creation. The question is not *whether* God rules over the kingdoms of the earth right now, but *how* he reigns over his church through saving grace and over the earthly powers through common grace.

As we deepen and correct our theological vision, we need also to deepen and correct our cultural vision. One notable example of this convergence is provided by Christian sociologist James Davison Hunter. In *To Change the World* he explains how cultures actually develop and the danger of thinking that direct and immediate attempts to change society are effective.[85] His own model of "faithful presence" seems to me to navigate wisely between transformationalism and apathy in our cultural engagement.

In the process of living out our ordinary discipleship, some may actually be called to remarkable acts of heroism and sacrificial leadership. In the course of their ordinary vocations, some may be extolled for their artistic brilliance, political labors, or scientific discoveries. It is crucial that Christians fulfill their various callings as salt and light in a tasteless and dark world. But the *kingdom of Christ* advances directly by the Spirit's miraculous gathering of a people around the Lamb to the glory of the Father through the ordinary means of grace. In addition to collapsing Christ and his work into the church and its labors, as well as collapsing the age to come into this present age, the transformational emphasis can blur the distinction between saving grace and common grace.

Loving Neighbors Is Tougher Than Loving Causes

An earlier point is worth repeating: it is easy to turn others into instruments of our ambition rather than loving them for their own sake, as fellow image bearers of God. They become supporting actors — if not props — in our life movie.

Loving actual neighbors through particular actions every day can be a lot more mundane as well as difficult than trying to transform culture. Regardless of the role or place in society to which God has assigned us by our calling, we are content. Our identity is already determined by our being "in Christ," not by our accomplishments. The measure of excellence is daily love for our neighbors during this time between Christ's two advents. Paul let the air out of inflated Corinthian egos when he reminded them:

> For consider your calling, brothers: not many of you were wise according to worldly standards, not many were powerful, not many were of noble birth. But God chose what is foolish in the world to

shame the wise; God chose what is weak in the world to shame the strong; God chose what is low and despised in the world, even things that are not, in order to bring to nothing the things that are, so that no human being might boast in the presence of God. (1 Cor 1:26–29)

It is evident from Paul's letters that the members of the Corinthian church were desperate to fit in with this culture. If Corinthian society placed a high value on style over substance, they would too. If lawsuits were common, then believers could also rush to court against each other. If sexual immorality was tolerated in society, it could be accommodated in the church. If strict socioeconomic divisions characterized civil life, you could have ranking positions in the church along the same lines.

Paul was not creating a new kind of elitism, where the truly spiritual were simply common laborers. If everyone were a janitor or carpenter, where would the other services—like ruling, study, and opening up large homes to fellow believers come from? Rather, Paul was targeting the envy and ambition of Corinthian believers who, with the help of the "super-apostles," had been imbibing a version of the prosperity gospel. To be sure, "not many" of the elect are the people who appear on the pages of *People* or in CNN interviews. But some are. The point is that their callings in the world do not give them any rank or privilege in the body of Christ. The key is to realize that the church is the place where the many members of the body, whoever they are, can be seen as equally crucial to the functioning of the whole body.

The idolatry of both the common person and the cultural elite results at least in part from losing sight of the proper orientation. This idolatry places a burden on the idols to come through for us or else suffer the devastating consequences of our collective disappointment. However, if God's pleasure and glory are ultimate and our neighbor's good the penultimate goal, we will engage culture in the way that God has gifted, prepared, and called us to do.

Evangelicals don't seem to care enough about "high culture" to invest in gospel operas or symphonies, but there is a longing for pop-cultural icons in our subculture. It is refreshing when someone with worldly fame refuses to be a "trophy Christian." Jon Foreman, lead singer for Switchfoot, was asked recently whether he considers his band "Christian." He replied:

> To be honest, this question grieves me because I feel that it represents a much bigger issue than simply a couple SF tunes. In true Socratic form, let me ask you a few questions: Does Lewis or Tolkien mention Christ in any of their fictional series? Are Bach's sonatas Christian? What is more Christ-like, feeding the poor, making furniture, cleaning bathrooms, or painting a sunset? ... The stance that a worship leader is more spiritual than a janitor is condescending and flawed. These different callings and purposes further demonstrate God's sovereignty.[86]

Of his own songs, Foreman adds, "None of these songs has been born again, and to that end there is no such thing as Christian music."

> No. Christ didn't come and die for my songs, he came for me. Yes. My songs are part of my life. I am a believer. Many of these songs talk about this belief. An obligation to say this or do that does not sound like the glorious freedom that Christ died to afford me.... (I've heard lots of people say Jesus Christ and they weren't talking about their redeemer.) You see, Jesus didn't die for any of my tunes.
>
> So there is no hierarchy of life or songs or occupation, only obedience. We have a call to take up our cross and follow. We can be sure that these roads will be different for all of us. Just as you have one body and every part has a different function, so in Christ we who are many form one body and each of us belongs to all the others. Please be slow to judge "brothers" who have a different calling.

In more concrete terms, the ideal of cultural transformation reflects a kind of collective ambition that overlooks ordinary faithfulness. I'm speaking to fellow ministers now. Think of the nurse who dragged herself out of bed to attend the means of grace after having worked a fifteen-hour shift. Pastors shouldn't feel guilty for not having cared for the physical needs of hundreds of neighbors in the hospital this last week. But why should they load down this nurse for failing to "live her faith" because she extended hours of neighbor love in her ordinary vocation rather than as an identifiable church-related "ministry"?

Or picture the parents of four children, one of whom has a rare blood disease. They both work tirelessly, one outside the home, loving and serving neighbors. They would like to have more friends and open up their home. Stirred by the opportunities and needs to volunteer for all sorts of good causes, they find that all of their time, energy, and resources go to caring for their family. Are they world changers? Should they be giving more time to "finding their ministry" in the church, so that the church can receive the credit for having an impact on the community?

I also think of the banker who came to church today. On Thursday he stretched the "best practices" a bit to extend a low-interest loan to a responsible but disadvantaged young family for their first home.

I picture the mom and dad who, though tired at the end of a busy day, read Scripture and pray with their children and then tuck them into bed with an imagination-building story. Some nights they forget or just cannot reach the day's finish line, but there's another day.

There is the Sunday school teacher who labors over the lesson in between working two jobs; the high schooler whose vocation is to learn, grow, and assume civic as well as church responsibilities; the struggling artist who makes us all stop to imagine ourselves and our place in the world a little differently; the lawyer who prosecutes the claims of justice and defends the rights of the accused—who just this past week offered pro bono hours to a victim who couldn't afford legal advice.

Now, all of these people are there before you. After their long week, filled with the hopes and fears of this present age, they are longing to hear something new, which they have not—could not—hear from the various institutions, media, and personalities they've encountered over the last six days. There are single people who are struggling with their relationships, wondering if they will always be lonely—and whether they're to blame. Others are struggling in their marriages, troubled by the way their children seem to ignore them, wrestling with the real possibility that one or both of them will be laid off at work.

You are Christ's ambassador, entrusted with his words. You dare not speak in his name, except for the fact that he authorized and commanded you to do so. What will you say? Are these folks your platoon for your own vision of having an important ministry that changes your community and your world? Is it not enough to "aspire to live quietly, and to mind your own affairs, and to work with your hands, as we instructed you, so that you may walk properly before outsiders and be dependent on no one" (1 Thess 4:11 – 12)? To love and serve our neighbors — especially those nearest to and most dependent on us — regardless of the burden?

Thank the Lord for the Wilberforces, who can truly be said to have changed the world. However, they did so in their worldly callings as believers and neighbors. It's what James Hunter calls "faithful presence." Moreover, they don't set out to change the world but to live out their identity in Christ where they are in all sorts of ordinary ways that sometimes turn out to present extraordinary moments of extraordinary opportunities for extraordinary service. There is that great scene in C. S. Lewis's *Chronicles of Narnia* when Aslan informs Caspian that he is about to become king in Narnia. "I don't think I'm ready," the young prince replies. Aslan responds, "It's for that very reason I know you are."

Ordinary People

We must beware of missing the value of the ordinary by seeing it as just one more means to greatness. True, there are many ordinary people who, precisely through their ordinary callings, sometimes make an extraordinary impact. Yet it is just as true that ordinary lives have an ordinary impact that is beautiful in its own right. The choice had to be made, hardly earth-shattering at the moment, between ignoring a child's complaint or taking her to the doctor. By choosing the latter, the busy mother saved her daughter's life.

Less catastrophic but no less dangerous is the choice to do

something big when something small is exactly what's called for in the moment. The habit of reading stories to children at bedtime is often tedious. Family and private devotions can be tedious as well. So too can daily homework be a chore for students, along with grading for teachers. Making rounds is often tedious for doctors and nurses. Yet daily faithfulness to these callings—more accurately, to God and the neighbors he has called us to serve—is precisely what enriches life.

We don't need another hero. We need a Savior, one who possessed "no form or majesty that we should look at him," and yet bore our sins (Isa 53:2–3). In fact, we need to be saved from our own hero worship, whether of ourselves or others. Jesus Christ never disappoints us because he is not simply someone to look up to because of his achievements, but is someone to trust because everything that he achieved was for us. And we need a communion of saints he has chosen and redeemed with us and for us. We need ordinary believers of every generation, race, and socioeconomic background to whom we're united by baptism to one Lord and one faith by one Spirit. We simply need ordinary pastors to deliver the word of life and its sacraments faithfully, elders to guide us to maturity, and deacons to help keep the temporal gifts circulating in the body.

The actual churches we know are often the most difficult places in the world, especially if we are creative, ambitious, and drawn toward novelty. The patient discipline of belonging to a community (preferably, the same local community) over a long period is difficult for those of us born after 1964. Church growth analysts often tell us that "brand loyalty" is a thing of the past and that churches will just have to catch up with that fact, just as they told us that niche churches grow faster because people like to worship with those who are like them (ethnically, generationally, and socioeconomically). We have Corinth written all over us.

The church in the abstract may be fine—the invisible company of God's elect. As the saying goes, "To dwell above with the saints in love—Oh, that will be glory! But to dwell below with the saints I know, well, that's a different story." We see ourselves as "on the move," making an impact—and we need others like us to be props or supporting actors in our movie. Contentment comes from knowing that the body of Christ is far greater than any of its members by itself. Even Christ considers himself incomplete until his whole body shares in his risen glory.

With that realization, what seemed like boring routine with boring people may actually take on a different aspect. Like a vast field, we are growing together into a harvest whose glory will only appear fully at the end of the age.

We need ordinary parents who care enough about the scads of small things each day that tend God's garden and direct them to their heavenly Father, the true hero "who so loved the world that he gave his only Son" (John 3:16).

Even in society, we need ordinary neighbors who play their part in the story. We need fewer Christians who want to stand apart from their neighbors, doing something that will really display God's kingdom in all of its glory. We need more Christians who take their place alongside believing and unbelieving neighbors in the daily gift exchange. The thief is not expected to become a monk or a famous evangelist, but to "labor, doing honest work with his own hands, so that he may have something to share with anyone in need" (Eph 4:28).

George Eliot concludes her classic novel *Middlemarch* with a profound eulogy for her lead character. Dorothea is an ordinary person who pursued ordinary interests that end up making a difference that no one might have expected:

> Her finely-touched spirit had still its fine issues, though they were not widely visible. Her full nature, like that of which Cyrus broke the strength, spent itself in channels which had no great name on the earth. But the effect of her being on those around her was incalculably diffusive: for the growing good of the world is partly dependent on unhistoric acts; and that things are not so ill with you and me as they might have been, is half owing to the number who lived faithfully a hidden life, and rest in unvisited tombs.[87]

168 | ordinary and content

Exercise

1. Do we tend to read the Bible — especially the Old Testament — as a catalog of heroes? How do our cultural assumptions of "the bold and the beautiful" shape our expectations of what we should find in these stories? How should we read these stories?

2. What are "ordinary" callings? What are the criteria we use to rank vocations in the church and in the world? Are they biblical?

3. Are we called by God in Scripture to transform culture? What are some of the weaknesses of this approach, both theologically and in our understanding of culture?

4. What do you think of the response by Switchfoot's lead singer, quoted in this chapter?

5. Consider/discuss some examples of the actual neighbors who cross your path each day. How do you love and serve them? Does it feel awkward to mention the ordinary "little" things, as if they're too trivial? Why or why not?

CHAPTER 9

God's ecosystem

Ecosystems are webs of interdependent life. No great sequoia can exist apart from its forest, and no forest can exist apart from its wider habitat. When the delicate balance is upset, the whole ecosystem is affected.

The church is not simply an institution with a systematic theology, but an organism with a form of life. In front of a computer, I'm in charge of what I want to learn and become—or at least I think I am. However, in the visible church I am not in front of anything. Rather, I'm in the middle of the action. I have some intimations, but I really don't know what I will become after the church is through with me. By being assimilated to its faith and practice, I do not lose my identity. On the contrary, I find it "in Christ," together with his body. The church is not just where disciples go; it's the place where disciples are made.

The Kingdom Is Like a Garden

Although it is a bit of a caricature, I think that there is some truth in the generalizations I'm about to make. The tendency in Roman Catholic theology is to view the kingdom of Christ as a cosmic ladder or tower, leading from the lowest strata to the hierarchy led by the pope. Anabaptists have tended to see the kingdom more as a monastery, a community of true saints called out of the world and a worldly church. Lutheran and Reformed churches tend sometimes to see the kingdom as a school, while evangelicals (at least in the United States) lean more toward seeing it as a market.

But God sees his kingdom as a garden. The dominance of organic metaphors for God's kingdom in Scripture is striking. Psalm 1:3–4 compares the heir of the covenant to "a tree planted by streams of water, that yields its fruit in its season, and its leaf does not wither." In contrast, "the wicked are not so, but are like chaff that the wind drives away." In the end, the ungodly will not stand in God's forest (1:5–6).

Israel is the vine of the Lord. Prophesying the exile, Isaiah sings a lament for the vineyard. The beloved planted it, tended it, and cared for it as his own. He kept looking for its success, "but it yielded wild grapes." Yahweh says, "And now, O inhabitants of Jerusalem and men of Judah, judge between me and my vineyard. What more was there to do for my vineyard, that I have not done?" So he will break down the hedge, wall, and watchtower. "I will make it a waste … I will also command the clouds that they rain no rain upon it" (Isa 5:2–6).

"I planted you a choice vine, wholly of pure seed," the Lord indicts through Jeremiah. "How then have you turned degenerate and become a wild vine?" (Jer 2:21).

Instead of being an oasis of life, the church had become assimilated to the surrounding desert of idolatry. With explicit echoes of Eden after the fall, the image we meet repeatedly in the prophets is of the gardener withdrawing, turning the oasis back to a barren land of thorns and tumbleweeds. It is not an invading army of pagans that has done this. "Many shepherds have destroyed my vineyard; they have trampled down my portion; they have made my pleasant portion a desolate wilderness" (Jer 12:10).

Yet the day is coming when the owner of the vineyard will send a faithful shepherd-gardener:

> I will heal their apostasy;
>   I will love them freely,
>   for my anger has turned from them.
> I will be like the dew to Israel;
>   he shall blossom like the lily;
>   he shall take root like the trees of Lebanon;

his shoots shall spread out;
    his beauty shall be like the olive,
    and his fragrance like Lebanon.
They shall return and dwell beneath my shadow;
    they shall flourish like the grain;
they shall blossom like the vine;
    their fame shall be like the wine of Lebanon.
O Ephraim, what have I to do with idols?
    It is I who answer and look after you.
I am like an evergreen cypress;
    from me comes your fruit. (Hos 14:4 – 8)

It is with these passages in mind, no doubt, that Jesus proclaims the Father as the gardener and himself as the vine. Already, John the Baptist announced, "Even now the axe is laid to the root of the trees. Every tree therefore that does not bear good fruit is cut down and thrown into the fire" (Matt 3:10).

The kingdom is like a sower who scattered seeds that fell in different soils. Some fell along the road and were eaten by birds. Others, lacking any root, "withered away" in the scorching sun. Some fell among thorns and were choked. "Other seeds fell on good soil and produced grain, some a hundredfold, some sixty, some thirty" (Matt 13:1 – 9). The kingdom is like a garden where an enemy sows weeds among the wheat. You can't tell the two apart until the harvest, so Jesus warns the disciples not to try to weed his garden until he returns (13:24 – 30).

> He put another parable before them, saying, "The kingdom of heaven is like a grain of mustard seed that a man took and sowed in his field. It is the smallest of all seeds, but when it has grown it is larger than all the garden plants and becomes a tree, so that the birds of the air come and make nests in its branches." (13:31 – 32)

Sometimes I hear pastors shrug off their responsibility by saying that there are different kinds of churches for different kinds of people. But our Lord has not allowed us this luxury. Some rest on the laurels of their orthodoxy. "Other churches evangelize people;

we teach them." That's like saying that others will scatter the seed, but our niche is the deep soil. Others rebuff criticisms of shallowness with D. L. Moody's famous quip: "I like my way of doing it better than your way of not doing it." But it is not enough to scatter the seed far and wide if it doesn't have fertile soil in which to grow.

Luke records the parable of the barren fig tree, planted in a vineyard. When the time came, he was surprised that it had no fruit, even after three years of tending it. (Jesus is referring to his own ministry). "Cut it down," the owner says to the vinedresser. "Why should it use up the ground?" The vinedresser answered, "Sir, let it alone this year also, until I dig around it and put on manure. Then if it should bear fruit next year, well and good; but if not, you can cut it down" (Luke 13:6–9). Jesus is giving Israel one last chance to repent, but then comes the judgment.

The theme runs throughout the parables. "For the kingdom of heaven is like a master of a house who went out early in the morning to hire laborers for his vineyard," Jesus says (Matt 20:1). In another parable, Jesus says that the master sent his two sons to work in the vineyard. One said he wouldn't go, but then he did; the other said he would go, but then he didn't. "Truly, I say to you, the tax collectors and the prostitutes go into the kingdom of God before you." The religious leaders rejected John the Baptist's call to repentance, while the moral outcasts embraced his message (Matt 21:28–32).

The next parable speaks of a master "who planted a vineyard and put a fence around it and dug a winepress in it and built a tower" — the echoes of Isaiah 5:1 are evident. Leasing it to tenants, he traveled out of the country. Near harvest time, the tenants beat and killed the master's servants he sent, one after another. Finally, the master sent his own son, but the tenants were even more eager to kill him so that they could have the vineyard to themselves. "Therefore, I tell you," Jesus says, "the kingdom of God will be taken away from you and given to a people producing its fruits" (Matt 21:33–43). Getting the point, the religious leaders wanted to arrest Jesus but feared what the crowds would do (21:45–46).

And then, on the Temple Mount that last week, Jesus lamented over Jerusalem like Jeremiah. He cursed the fig tree: " 'May no fruit ever come from you again!' And the fig tree withered at once" (Matt 21:18–19). It is not surprising that these parables are placed in the last week, on the Temple Mount, amid straightforward prophecies announcing the destruction of the temple and the end of the old covenant era.

Now Jesus is the temple and he is the vine.

> I am the true vine, and my Father is the vinedresser. Every branch in me that does not bear fruit he takes away, and every branch that does bear fruit he prunes, that it may bear more fruit. Already you are clean because of the word that I have spoken to you. Abide in me, and I in you. As the branch cannot bear fruit by itself, unless it abides in the vine, neither can you, unless you abide in me. I am the vine; you are the branches. Whoever abides in me and I in him, he it is that bears much fruit, for apart from me you can do nothing. (John 15:1–5)

United to Christ through faith, we are simultaneously united to our fellow branches. We are not the vine, but a branch inextricably connected to the tree of life.

What are some of the common threads we can draw together from Jesus' organic analogy of his kingdom? First, it is *his* kingdom. Second, there is no personal relationship with Christ, the Vine, apart from his church, the branches. Third, the growth of this kingdom (and each member of it) is slow. Who would ever have imagined that a tiny mustard seed would become a massive tree with branches filling the earth? Yet it isn't something you can measure day by day. Fourth, it takes a lot of work. The gardener is always doing something to tend the vine in view of his harvest.

How Does God's Garden Grow?

There are no shortcuts. All the Miracle Grow in the world cannot compensate for honest toil. The soil has to be right: deep and rich enough to nourish the seed. Thornbushes have to be pulled out so that they do not choke the growing plant. One minute he is planting, the next he is watering, trimming, digging around the roots, and fertilizing. The wild environment is always trying to claim the vine.

Now imagine what would happen if the gardener, impatient with the slow progress, kept pulling up the plants, transplanting them somewhere else. Or spread the soil broadly to increase his acreage, but without sufficient depth? Or, distracted by immediate growth, ignored the pests that devour the leaves? Or, in his zeal for the vine's purity, accidentally cut off living vines that he thought were dead? This in sharp contrast with the Master of the vineyard, who does not break off a bruised branch but nurses it back to full health (Isa 42:3 with Matt 12:20).

Alongside the organic analogy is the architectural one: the kingdom as a building. In fact, they are often combined in one mixed metaphor—and it works! The picture is a building that is alive and growing. Here's how Paul describes it:

> So then you are no longer strangers and aliens, but you are fellow citizens with the saints and members of the household of God, built on the foundation of the apostles and prophets, Christ Jesus himself being the cornerstone, in whom the whole structure, being joined together, grows into a holy temple in the Lord. In him you also are being built together into a dwelling place for God by the Spirit. (Eph 2:19–22)

At his ascension, Christ began raining gifts down on his church and sent his Spirit to distribute them to all the saints. All share equally in the gift of Christ and his Spirit: "one Lord, one faith, one baptism," he says. "But grace was given to each one of us according to the measure of Christ's gift." The gifts Paul singles out here for the purpose of his argument are prophets and apostles and now "the evangelists, the pastors and teachers," who bring us all to maturity. Through their ministry they are "building up the body of Christ, until we all attain to the unity of the faith and of the knowledge of the Son of God ... to the measure of the stature of the fullness of Christ, so that we may no longer be children, tossed to and fro by the waves and carried about by every wind of doctrine, by human cunning, by craftiness in deceitful schemes" (Eph 4:4–14).

As they say, Rome wasn't built in a day—and neither is the church or any local expression of it. Nor is a believer. Each of us is a living stone inserted to a living building with Christ as its cornerstone. Like a tree, the building is growing up and growing out. Like branches, stones are always being added. But it takes time. And most of the things that construction workers do on an average day may seem fairly humdrum: hammering, drilling, marking, cutting, and so forth. There is a lot in between the ceremonial turning of the first shovel of dirt and the cutting of the ribbon. Not until Christ returns will the church's ribbon be cut, unveiling the everlasting sanctuary of God.

Isn't it striking that the Lord selected agricultural analogies? The other big ones are pretty close to that root metaphor. The church is the pasture with Christ as the good Shepherd, who provides undershepherds to guide us in our pilgrimage. Just as the soil is important for his plants, as Jesus emphasized, so is the pasture for sheep. We not only feed on doctrine, as if we were only independent minds, but on nutrients that only a particular environment can produce.

Perhaps the most dominant analogy for evangelicals over many generations now is "fire." There are "revival fires," God is "blazing" and "consuming" and "burning throughout the world." In Scripture, God is "a consuming fire," but this is intended to be disconcerting (Heb 12:29). The good news is that we have not come to Mount Sinai, with blazing fire, but to Mount Zion, with a festival of heavenly hosts celebrating the saving work of Christ (12:12–24).

But what about Pentecost, with flames appearing above each person? In context, the flames represent witness to Christ, not the zeal of the witnesses. We hope that witness will be passionate, but that's not the point. The more deeply rooted we are in the Word of God, the more our witness will be authentic and imbued with personal conviction. However, the power of God unto salvation is not our passion for God, but the passion he has exhibited toward us sinners by sending his own Son to redeem us.

None of these other metaphors has the deep and broad scriptural resonance that the organic analogy enjoys; our churches and families need desperately to recover that picture in actual practice.

The Sabbath as God's Greenbelt

Imagine living in a village where everyone walked to the parish church, returned home to family discussions of the sermon, then rested, and returned to the evening service. In the afternoon there might be a visit to the local nursing home or orphanage for works of mercy.

Of course, the reality was never uniform. Besides hypocrites, there have always been legalists who turned the festival into a funeral. Christians have always struggled to keep the day focused on the age to come that is breaking into this present evil age. Nevertheless, the very fact that those who didn't take it seriously had to pretend that they did (or at least not cause offenses in public) shows how local culture shapes us as individuals.

The practice of worshiping on the day Jesus rose from the dead—the first day of the week—goes back to the time of the apostles (Matt 28:1; Mark 16:2; Luke 24:1; John 20:1; Acts 20:7; 1 Cor 16:2; Rev 1:10). However, practicing the Lord's Day is extremely difficult in our society today. Few neighbors treat it as a "greenbelt" in time. Many, including Christians, look bewildered when you decline an invitation to a soccer game during morning or evening worship. In fact, many *church* activities on Sunday have less to do with inculcating the faith than with providing "safe" things for kids to do.

Beyond this, a growing number of churches offer a menu of services on other days for convenience. In addition to a Saturday evening service, one may elect to participate in a small group with people in our stage of life or interests.

Setting aside the ordinary callings and pastimes of the week, our calling on the Lord's Day is to share, together with our coheirs, in the powers of the age to come. It is not by simply *emptying* the day with a list of rules, but by *filling* it with treasure hunting, that the Christian Sabbath orients us, our families, and our fellow saints to our heavenly citizenship. However, everyone around you sees it as the ideal day for a trip to the mall, sports, and other entertainments. Whatever fills our Sundays fills our hearts throughout the week. The Lord's Day is not a prison but a palace. It is a wonderful gift to turn off the devices that interrupt our daily schedules and to push our roots down into the fertile soil that produces trees in God's garden. It is a delight to set aside our normal associations with friends and coworkers—even non-Christian family members—in order to commiserate with fellow heirs of the kingdom concerning the news we've heard about the age to come.

"Reduce, Reuse, Recycle"

This formula has become part of our psyche now. But there was a time when many of us considered it an onerous demand. Eventually, we changed some habits in the interest of long-term sustainability. It's not a bad formula for God's garden.

We need to *reduce* the distractions and voracious consumption. Many things that we do as "something more" aren't bad in themselves. Yet collectively they contribute to a whirling buzz of confusion that keeps us from fixing our eyes on Christ and his kingdom and his ordinary means of grace. We never move on from the gospel to something else. J. I. Packer and Gary A. Parrett put it well: "We believe, rather, that it is imperative to think of moving on from the 'milk' of the Gospel to the 'meat' of the Gospel. For in fact the Gospel is more profound and multifaceted than our finite minds can ever grasp. We never move on *from* the Gospel; we move on *in* the Gospel."[88]

We also need to *reuse* the resources that God has given us from the past. Forms that frame the public service—common prayer, praise, and confession—are ways of thoughtfully drawing on Scripture so that Christ's word dwells in all of us richly. A trellis does not make a vine grow, but it does make it grow in the right direction. The Psalms train our hearts to pour out sorrowful laments as well as joyful praise, to recall God's faithfulness in the past as well as to invoke his faithfulness for the future, to confess our sins and to profess our faith in the one who absolves us by his word of pardon. In Acts 2:42, we read that the early believers gathered not only for the apostles' teaching, fellowship, and the breaking of the bread, but also for "the prayers." Corporate prayers of confession, intercession, and praise would have been familiar to Jews raised in the synagogue.

We also need to *recycle*. This involves two moves: returning to the sources and adapting them to our time and place. Recycling should not be equivalent to simply repeating slogans and formulas. We need to exercise discernment as we evaluate older forms and practices, but we do not have to invent everything ourselves. Older forms, songs, and prayers are not better because they are old, but because they are family treasures in the attic. We need to ensure that our forms actually communicate with people in our time and place, but we do not have to change everything with each generation.

God even recycles ministers. They come and go, but the ministry is the gift that keeps on giving. Carl Trueman wisely reminds us:

> The elite watchmaker Patek Philippe had a slogan at one time that was something like this: "You never really own a Patek Philippe; you merely look after it for the next generation." Thus it is with churches, in terms of the vibrancy of their life and their orthodoxy. Those privileged enough to be involved in the appointment of their own successors, or those who can merely shape the nature of the session [local council of elders] which will oversee the search, need to make sure they make the right choices. They do not own the church; they are merely looking after her for the next generation.[89]

Recall my example above of a gardener who plants a tree and then in restless activity uproots and transplants it every few weeks. That tree will likely never bear fruit and will probably wither and die. Why then do we seem to think that churches need to imitate the perpetual innovation of Microsoft instead of the patient care of a good gardener?

Chasing the latest fad for spiritual growth, church growth, and cultural impact, we eventually forget both how to reach the lost and how to keep the reached. The ordinary means of grace become yesterday's news. Like pay phones, so we are told by emergent entrepreneurs, ordinary churches may still be around here and there, but nobody uses them. In olden days believers may have gathered for "the apostles' teaching and the fellowship ... the breaking of the bread and the prayers," but that was before iPads. In past generations, Christ's fruit-bearing vines may have been tended with daily family disciplines of catechism, Bible reading, and prayer, but with *my* schedule? And to say that the apostolic method of church growth—in breadth as well as depth—is preaching, teaching, baptism, the Lord's Supper, and accountability to elders is likely to provoke the response: "Are you *serious?*"

Christ's undershepherds and gardeners are burning out today at an alarming rate. Many of them identify unrealistic expectations as a key reason. A lot of them, no doubt, entered seminary because they wanted to serve alongside Christ in his vineyard. They wanted to scatter, water, and tend his vines. Yet even in seminary they may have encountered a bewildering array of options for niche ministries, while they had hoped to master Hebrew and Greek, church history, and various branches of biblical studies and theology. They wanted to be "a worker who has no need to be ashamed, rightly handling the word of truth" (2 Tim 2:15). But they were being prepared for the many pressures they will encounter in the real churches of our day. Then they discover that this is in fact the case. They are expected to be CEO, therapist, entertainer, coach, and best friend.

In the face of these pressures, pastors and elders—as well as the rest of the congregation—need to get off the treadmill and ask what really matters. What is Christ's commission for his ambassadors? What are the qualifications and job description of church officers that we find in the writings of the apostles? If we do not reduce, reuse, and recycle, returning first of all to our biblical sources, we will discover at some point, if we haven't already, that the present state of ministry is unsustainable for pastors and those they serve.

Personal Disciplines

In its healthier eras, church disciplines were firmly in place. In spite of persecution and milder disincentives to conversion, the ancient church pursued a pretty rigorous program of teaching and evaluation that preceded baptism and membership of adult converts. After all, Gentiles at least came from paganism.

Perhaps we do not really think that Americans are pagans. That is our first mistake. In any case, the ancient church grew and thrived throughout the Roman Empire against all odds through careful, deliberate, and formal practices of catechesis. Catechesis is simply instruction, identified especially with a common form of sound words in question-and-answer format. New Christians and children learn these summaries of the faith as older saints continually deepen their understanding through these shared statements. We grow up together, being of the same mind and heart.

These practices fell away rather sharply with the annexation of Christ to the Roman Empire under Constantine. They became more difficult to sustain in the medieval church for a host of reasons. Eventually, the gospel was taken for granted. It was simply assumed that if you were a European with a heartbeat, you were a Christian.

The Reformation sought to recover these ancient practices, although the assumptions of "Christendom" persisted. Luther wrote his Small and Large Catechisms, while the Heidelberg Catechism and the Westminster Shorter and Larger Catechisms have shaped the common faith of generations of Reformed believers on every continent. Each person was called upon to trust in Christ, to learn the faith, and to profess it publicly in the congregation. Elders took responsibility to look after the flock, to visit their homes regularly, and to rebuke, correct, instruct, and encourage. Deacons looked after their temporal needs, so that nobody was without the necessities of life.

Needless to say, this church discipline has fallen on hard times in the land that Dietrich Bonhoeffer aptly described as "Protestantism without the Reformation." In a land that increasingly defies any external authorities, personal faith and responsibility now mean that no human being—or even council of human beings—can interfere with the individual's personal relationship with God. The United States is the first nation in history to make personal choice the heart of its creed. In this the churches are not only the influenced but also influencers, especially as the sovereign will of the individual over-runs all levies that have been formed by both classical and biblical traditions.

Among the myriad programs, books, and sermons on disciple-ship and disciple-making, how many give priority to the church's role and the importance of submission to the teaching and guidance of those whom Christ has placed over us?

Even the ordinary disciplines of family devotions seem to be vanishing. For centuries, believers were raised with prayer, singing, instruction, and Bible reading with the family each morning and evening. The Reformers and their spiritual heirs not only wrote cat-echisms for this purpose, but books with each day's readings, prayers, and songs. They knew that, as central as it was, the public ministry was weekly, and it needed to be supplemented and supported by daily habits.

As church and family disciplines were subordinated to private dis-ciplines, the burden of growing in the faith was placed almost exclu-sively on the individual. If do-it-yourself discipleship was the order of the day not that long ago, what is striking today is the extent to which even personal disciplines seem to be receding. It seems to me that there is increasingly less interest in personal prayer and meditation on God's Word than in any time since the Middle Ages. It suggests that when public disciplines (especially the weekly service) lose their hold on us, family and private disciplines are sure to follow.

We need to rethink our priorities here, and recovering an appre-ciation for the ordinary is at least one step in that direction. We grow by ordinary, daily, habitual practices. The weekly service of the Word and sacrament, along with its public confession of sin and faith, the prayers, and praise, are the fountain that flows into our homes and private rooms throughout the week. It is all of these disciplines—public, family, and private—that we need to recover. They may seem ordinary. In fact, they are! But that is precisely how God's garden grows each day.

Emerging Branches

When personal choice is the key concept, the status of your kids in the kingdom is not exactly clear. Sometimes there is even a fear of parents "interfering" with the child's personal relationship with Jesus. Some of our more outspoken neighbors take it one step further, wondering whether we are abusing children by "indoctrinating" them before they can choose a religion (or no religion) for themselves.

The problem is that our children increasingly have not been given enough of the Christian faith even to apostatize from it properly. If you want to talk about brainwashing children, it is not churches that are the best examples. One marketing professor explains, "There are only two ways to increase customers. Either you switch them to your brand or you grow them from birth." The president of a chain of children's specialty stores says, "All of these people understand something that is very basic and logical, that if you own this child at an early age, you can own this child for years to come. Companies are saying, 'Hey, I want to own the kid younger and younger and younger.'" A General Mills executive adds, "When it comes to targeting kid consumers, we at General Mills follow the Proctor & Gamble model of 'cradle to grave.' We believe in getting them early and having them for life." Finally, the president of a leading ad agency declares, "Advertising at its best is making people feel that without their product, you're a loser. Kids are very sensitive to that.... You open up emotional vulnerabilities, and it's very easy to do with kids because they're the most emotionally vulnerable."[90]

We dare not imagine that our children are neutral choosers any more than we are. They are already being cultivated to take their place in the succession of contractual consumers. Are our churches and homes transplanting them to God's garden? Are our vision statements and strategies modeled on the Great Commission, aiming at sustainable growth in both breadth and depth? Are we incorporating people into the covenant of grace, or marketing contracts for religious goods and services? It is not simply that we are selling something different from Proctor & Gamble, but that because it is the gospel from heaven, we are not *selling* anything at all. It is not the values of the company that should pervade our strategy sessions and fill our hearts with concern, but the eternal value of being in Christ, living in the Vine, adding branches through our witness, and growing in his garden until he returns for the harvest.

In an interesting article in *The Atlantic*, Larry Alex Taunton reflected on his survey of young atheists.[91] He discerned a common thread in the testimonies. Many were raised in churches, most of them evangelical, but they were not really planted deeply in the faith.

One person, Phil, was just discovering things when his youth pastor was fired for not drawing in enough kids. It was all about "handholding and kumbaya," said one "with a look of disgust." He said, "I missed my old youth pastor. He actually knew the Bible." These were not the acerbic faces of the New Atheism, like Richard Dawkins, but young people who seemed genuinely disappointed that they couldn't find answers to their big questions.

A composite picture emerged. The young atheists interviewed had attended church, but said that "the mission and message of their churches were vague." They "felt their churches offered superficial answers to life's difficult questions." "Serious-minded, they often concluded that church services were largely shallow, harmless, and ultimately irrelevant. As Ben, an engineering major at the University of Texas, so bluntly put it: 'I really started to get bored with church.'" They also "expressed their respect for those ministers who took the Bible seriously," who really were convinced of its truth even where it clashed with public opinion.

Giving our attention again to "best practices" in spiritual gardening, our homes and churches need to become more child-friendly without being child-centered. I share Ivy Beckwith's concern that "by prohibiting children from the worship of their faith community we are, in effect, prohibiting them from an important piece of their spiritual development and denying them the opportunity to learn how to worship God in the tradition of their community."[92]

Kenda Creasy Dean, a Methodist minister and Princeton Seminary professor of youth ministry and culture, was involved in the National Study of Youth and Religion (NSYR). A massive sociological project over three years (2003–2005), the NSYR's conclusions were somewhat ominous. Exploring these conclusions, Dean's *Almost Christian* begins, "Here is the gist of what you are about to read: American young people are fine, theoretically, with religious faith—but it does not concern them very much, and it is not durable enough to survive long after they graduate from high school. One more thing: we're responsible."[93]

Chiefly, she says, young people raised in the church often don't feel connected to it. They do not feel connected on the theological level. In other words, they don't know what they believe or why. They aren't even sure *what* they doubt, and even if they are, they aren't terribly convinced that the people they know could relieve those doubts. In any case, it just does not matter that much. They also do not feel connected at the social level.

Unintentionally, the net effect of youth ministry has been largely to alienate younger generations from the ordinary life and ministry of the church. Dean argues that in so radically shifting from traditional forms—such as including young people in the regular service, using a catechism to teach the basics, and reinforcing the faith at home—we have unwittingly undermined their faith.

Kate Murphy agrees. She tells the story of Jonathan. Sara, an elderly saint, had just died and Jonathan, a teenager, asked if he could take her place in the choir that Sunday. Not only did he feel connected to Sara; he felt connected to the church and shared its grief over this loss. That just doesn't happen in youth-group ghettos. "I think I've done youth ministry with integrity," Kate says. "But I may have been unintentionally disconnecting kids from the larger body of Christ. The young people at my current congregation—a church that many families would never join because 'it doesn't have anything for youth'—are far more likely to remain connected to the faith and become active church members as adults, because that's what they already are and always have been."[94] We need to rethink how we minister to our youth, how we connect them to the "cloud of witnesses." At the curricular level, I suggest that we eschew "child-centered" educational methods in favor of "content-centered" instruction.

Having four of my own, I understand the difficulty of having children in church. Our church has a cry room, where parents can still participate in the service to some extent, but it is a chore. Yet isn't it a chore of parenthood? Eventually the parents decide when they will move out of the cry room. It is remarkable how early children learn habits of sitting and listening. Even if they doodle and daydream for a couple of years, these habits of participation in the communion of saints are like a trellis. These habits do not guarantee that everyone will eventually respond in faith, but they do make for better hearing of that gospel through which faith takes root and grows in our hearts.

Besides the concern for parents, many Christians wonder if it is good for children to have them in the regular service. After all, they cannot understand what is going on. But imagine saying that you're not going to have toddlers sit at the table for meals with the family because they do not understand the rituals or manners. Or keeping infants isolated in a nursery with nothing but mobiles and squeaky toys because they cannot understand the dialogue of the rest of the family around them. We know, instinctively, that it's important for our children to acquire language and the ordinary rituals of their family environment in order to become mature. Or imagine keeping our teens from their grandparents' funerals because they don't understand it. We take them precisely so they will, knowing that our patience (and theirs) will be rewarded in later years and that the event will itself be an opportunity for maturity. Jesus grew in wisdom and knowledge. He learned the Psalter and the rhythms of the synagogue liturgy. When, as a young adult, he took up the Isaiah scroll to read about himself, he knew exactly where to roll it.

At the *grammar* stage, children are simply absorbing the language of Zion: the terms and "the pattern of the sound words" (2 Tim 1:13) that we share with the wider body of Christ through the ages. I think that we are sometimes too worried about "imposing" our faith on our children. After all, it's a personal relationship with Jesus, and we do not want to interfere with their free will. We don't think this way about the other things that they are learning by rote at this stage. We do not upbraid teachers for "imposing" the alphabet or multiplication table. Our moral sentiments are not offended when parents correct poor grammar. Furthermore, recall the explicit agenda expressed by marketing executives at the beginning of this chapter. Children are being catechized every day, but in what?

The ecumenical creeds and evangelical confessions are an important place to start, and if they learn these summaries in the home and in Sunday school, they will be more likely to join the rest of the body in confessing that faith publicly in the service each week. In fact, the Protestant Reformers recovered the ancient practice of instruction through a catechism. With its question-and-answer format, these catechisms teach the core of our catholic and evangelical faith.[95]

Then, as young people approach the *logic* stage in their development, they see the relations between various doctrines and can even begin to make some of their own connections. No longer simply parroting the answers that they learned by heart, they are now stepping into the story themselves and thinking through the implications. Questioning things is part and parcel of being a teenager. Instead of seeing this as a threat, we should welcome it as the path to personal profession of the faith.

It is precisely in asking questions—even giving some push-back—that we come truly to understand and to own the faith. Sadly, many parents and church leaders are in greatest danger of "imposing" their faith in these teen years in reaction against a questioning process that is mistaken for rebellion. This is not the "grammar" stage, and the church should be the safest place for inquiring minds to discover the best answers to questions they will have into adulthood.

Now, as they pack off for college, this catechetical formation will hopefully have played a large part in their own faith. It will also help them to be "prepared to make a defense to anyone who asks you for a reason for the hope that is in you; yet do it with gentleness and respect" (1 Pet 3:15).

But it's not only a matter of the right content and method of instruction. We also grow more and more in our union with Christ and his body through intentional and structured social practices ordained by Christ. Recall the ordinary weekly ministry in Acts 2: "So those who received his word were baptized, and there were added that day about three thousand souls. And they devoted themselves to the apostles' teaching and the fellowship, to the breaking of bread and the prayers" (2:41–42).

What place does my baptism have even now in daily life? What does this tell me about who my closest relatives are? Even more than husband and wife, we are brother and sister in Christ. Even more than children in a natural family, we are coheirs and adopted children together with the Father, in the Son, by the Spirit. Am I the beneficiary of and submissive "to the teaching and the fellowship" of Christ's undershepherds? What is being given to me, done for me and to me, in the Lord's Supper, as I am drawn out of my self-enclosed cocoon to cling to Christ in faith and to my brothers and sisters in love?

How do "the prayers" shape my own participation in Christ and his body, so that even when I pray in private or with my family, I am still doing so with Christ and his church? Some of the prayers are sung as well. Do these songs make "the word of Christ dwell in you richly" (Col 3:16)? Are youth group trips planned in sync with the wider church activities, or do they regularly draw the young people away from the church, even on occasion the ordinary public service on the Lord's Day?

Wherever possible, the pastor should lead the profession or confirmation classes. This helps to connect them once more to the wider body. I find it intriguing that despite their busy schedules, Luther, Bucer, Calvin, Knox, and other Reformers taught the catechism every week to the youth. It makes a profound impression on a young person to be taken so seriously by the minister of the whole flock. The fact that the same minister who directs them through their questioning at this stage is also leading the whole congregation in worship each week has a quiet but powerful integrity. If our young people leave for college without having been grounded in the truth and wrestling honestly with their doubts, we shouldn't be surprised that they sleep in on Sunday in college. As it is, I fear that we are sending many young people into a battle unarmed.

Is there still a place for ministry to youth? Absolutely — in fact, that is the point of the preceding argument. But is there a place for youth ministries and youth ministers? There are some terrific examples of youth ministries that focus on integration rather than segregation.[96] I think it is helpful to think of youth ministry as parachurch. Ideally, such ministries fulfill their calling of coming alongside (*para*) the church, to lead people into the church. Depending on various factors, this may be done best by calling a youth minister or by designating an elder to oversee the coordination of various events.

For instance, what if there were at least as many trips to nursing homes and other care facilities as to theme parks? And more discussions focused on the actual content of the faith than on the important but often overdone talks on dating, relationships, and self-esteem? I'm not convinced that there is a single answer here, and I'm not opposed to targeted ministry to young people. The question is whether we are contributing to or detracting from the church's mission to build up each member into one body, in connection with its living Head.

With the gospel, even this world takes on a different light. We begin to see more colors, to taste more flavors, to enjoy this life in ways that before seemed impossible.

Yet it is especially in Christ's body that the new world — the real world — comes alive to us. Observing the health, wealth, and happiness of the wicked, Asaph confesses, "My feet almost stumbled" (Ps 73:2). But then he entered the sanctuary and everything began to fall into place (73:16 – 28). Similarly, every time we hear God's Word, witness a baptism, receive the Supper, and join in common confession, prayer, and praise, the familiar world of the work week seems like a passing shadow. Its siren songs become faint as we hear the strains of a stirring symphony approaching. We begin to taste morsels of the wedding feast that is being prepared. Even through these ordinary means, something extraordinary has arrived, is arriving, will arrive. But we wait for it patiently.

Exercise

1. Discuss the agricultural and organic imagery Scripture gives us for the kingdom of Christ. How does this differ from other ways we think about it?
2. How does God's garden grow? Can you see this in concrete ways in your own life, family and church? What are some of the ways we tend to undermine this view of growth in Christ?
3. What are your personal disciplines like? Why are they important?
4. Evaluate some of the major ways that children are nurtured in the faith at church. Are these methods healthy/unhealthy? Why?

CHAPTER 10

stop dreaming and love your neighbor

In a commencement address in 1987, comedian and educator Bill Cosby took aim at the usual hype that has become the staple of such events. "You're not going to change the world, so don't try." The best thing you can do is to live each day with integrity and responsibility, he advised, as laughter turned to nervous chuckles and shifting in the seats. Stop being narcissistic about your "dream," getting everyone else to fit into it, Cosby also told Temple University grads in 2012. "You've got plenty of time, but don't dream through it. Wake up!"[97]

From childhood we're told that we can be anything we want to be, do anything we want to do, make of ourselves whatever we dream. We often miss the trees for the forest, looking for ambitious causes instead of actual people God has sent into our lives that moment, hour, day, or year.

Meant to inspire us, this constant message can actually paralyze us with anxiety. This chapter focuses on the importance of staying at our posts to which God has called us: as children, parents, extended family, neighbors, coworkers, and citizens. We need to stop looking for extraordinary callings to give meaning to our lives, which often encourage us to think of others as tools in our self-crafting. It's not "the needy" who need us, but particular people—many of whom we come across every day. Our neighbor is right in front of us. Recall that closing line I've mentioned in chapter 8 from George Eliot's *Middlemarch*: "The growing good of the world is partly dependent on unhistoric acts; and that things are not so ill with you and me as they might have been, is half owing to the number who lived faithfully a hidden life, and rest in unvisited tombs."

You Go, Girl!

The intensity of the prepping for adult success, especially by Boomer and Buster parents, has caused a lot of stress for boys, but girls may be a larger casualty. We are ambivalent about the role of women — in the home, in the church, and in society. This tension gets transferred to children, especially girls. On the one hand, they're expected to be preparing for Proverbs 31 wifehood/motherhood. That's pressure enough. But on the other hand, they're also encouraged on many hands to be everything a boy can be, to do everything boys can do. Schizophrenic ourselves on these questions, we may even place both of these contradictory and unlivable expectations on our girls.

Trying to live up to their own dreams and those that society and parents have placed on them, many young women are putting off marriage and especially children. In many cases, these come along at just the wrong time: when young professional women are in full swing with their career. The women who get squeezed out as slackers are those who decide at the outset that they want to be a wife and mother. They have to brace themselves for the response at high school or college reunions when they say that they're "a stay-at-home mom." "Seriously, though," the former roommate's face reads even if the words don't come out, "don't you have a job?" And this is what they often hear from fellow believers!

I want to be careful here. I am not one of those guys who wants his daughter to live on a prairie making her own butter. Especially since World War II, when women helped achieve victory by their heroic labor in factories and even in various roles in the armed forces, an entire sector of the economy has been driven toward time-saving technologies for the home. Part of the rationale at least was that women could be liberated from domestic toil to pursue other interests and even vocations. I could not have gone to college without my mom's work outside the home. Wives work tirelessly outside the home to put their husbands through the seminary where I teach. Unlike previous eras, churches assume far less of a burden for their young aspirants to the holy office. So they are hardly in a position to make these dedicated spouses feel more guilty for picking up the slack.

Women do have callings outside the home. They are not only wives and mothers, but also friends and neighbors cultivating culture at the most local level in countless ways. Many also have additional callings for which they have been educated and trained. Like their male counterparts, they have student debt and expectations of making good use of their education. Avoiding legalism and antinomianism, we need wisdom. Each case will differ from others. It is for single women and couples themselves to decide what is best in their case, drawing on biblical principles and the specifics of their own situation.

But what I do want to challenge is the particular stress of being "superwoman." I have already addressed the more cross-gender issues of ambition and restlessness. These characteristics pressure both men and women to make their work an idol. In reaction against this danger, many parents are expected to focus on the family, but with extraordinary expectations. Often, fathers are stressed out as they try to balance foreign and domestic vocations. They have to be warlords, raising Daniels and Deborahs in the Lord's army. However, much of this expectation falls especially on mothers. Now the family can become an idol, even if you work full-time at home. So in addition to being a cab driver, shuttling the kids between various activities, Mom has to be a pastor, teacher (expert on everything), volunteer, social worker, and chef. In a high-risk world, it's all up to Supermom. Conservatives and progressives have different ways of substituting ambitions of greatness for attentiveness to the ordinary.

Nowhere is the ordinary more important to culture and yet less valuable in our society than in relation to motherhood. I'm not saying anything pro or con here about women working outside the home.

I'm only suggesting that the burdens we place on women — even from childhood — make them anxious about life and drive them to expect dissatisfaction with the normal and everyday aspects of life that are so crucial for the development of deep roots, wisdom, and nurture for the whole family.

Many of the things that mothers do in the home are not even measurable, much less stupendously satisfying on a daily basis. Much of it can be tedious, repetitive, and devoid of the intellectual stimulation found in adult company. In a myriad of ways, the daily calling of dying to self is felt more acutely by mothers. What they need is fewer guilt trips and expectations and more encouragement as they invest in ordinary tasks that yield long-term dividends.

In other vocations, we can often follow best practices, with the general expectation of successes that can be evident to us and to others. Yet there is no promotion in motherhood. Successes are measured in years, not days or even months, and you can never be quite sure of all the things you did each day that made a difference. Mothers stand at the core of that gift exchange as it radiates into ever-wider concentric circles, from the home to the neighborhood and church, and to society at large. Precisely because they are gifts and not commodities, domestic labors sustain communities that cannot be measured or valued in the marketplace. That is their strength, not their weakness.

Everything that I have said about motherhood has obvious applications to fathers as well. Ambition encourages us to make two mistakes. First, we become consumed with our work. Second, we try to make up for it by "quality time": major investments in family vacations. We need to take the pressure off of both parents, let them take a breath, and, resting in God's grace, let them revel in the ordinary chat in the car, the normal conversation over family devotions, and the countless moments that add up. Our families, including us, do not need more quality time, but more quantity time. That's when most of the best things happen. We think that such events are spontaneous — and to a certain extent they are. But they are really the things that bubble up when people are living ordinary lives together.

People versus Projects

I have already quoted the first answer of the Westminster Shorter Catechism: "The chief end of man is to glorify God and to enjoy him forever." It's sometimes easier for us to glorify God (or try to) than to enjoy him. Even with the best motives and intentions, we can become so busy seeking to bring praise to God through what we do for him that we don't delight in him for who he is and for what he has given us.

The same goes for our neighbors. We can be so caught up in doing things for our neighbors that we use them as service projects. Their needs—even misfortune—provide an opportunity for us to tweak our self-image and "grow as a person." These aren't wrong in themselves as by-products, but there is a danger of turning other people into instruments for our own selfish ends.

Do we *enjoy* our neighbor? It's a lot easier to serve a neighbor than to enjoy him or her. It's a lot easier to see me and my service as a gift to someone less fortunate, without seeing a "needy" person as a gift to me. In addition, it's a lot easier to enjoy the "neighbor" I'll serve in the soup line—whom I'll probably not see again, at least for more than five or ten minutes at a time—than the one who actually lives next door and wakes me up after midnight with wild parties. It's easier to pour myself into a service project for the needy than it is to give a little more to my wife and kids. That's ordinary. I can't see the impact of the dozen or so little conversations, corrections, laughs, and tasks that happen in a day—or even a week, month, perhaps even a year. I can't measure the ordinary stuff. But I can measure (supposedly) how many souls were saved or how many people were fed or how much money came in for a special project.

We look at the work of someone like Mother Theresa from the end point, as the Nobel Prize-winning figure who founded an order of nuns spread across India and around the world to serve the poor. However, she described her own life in terms of countless decisions and actions that hardly seem revolutionary on a daily scale. She learned to help the person she was with at the moment—actual neighbors, not "the poor" in general, but people created in God's image who needed something particular that she had to give.

A fellow used to pass a massive construction site on his way to work. One day he stopped and asked people what they were doing. One worker answered, "Hauling dirt." Another replied, "Cutting stones." Standing up straight, a third man replied cheerfully, "I'm building a cathedral." The goal was extraordinary and it was this that motivated what seemed on the surface to be nothing more than dull routine. We need to think like that. We do not need to be Michelangelo to take delight in helping build the scaffold that he used to paint the Sistine Chapel. Not only in the ministry, but in all vocations, some plant, some water, but the Lord gives the increase.

Two Kinds of Sacrifice

The Old Testament law provided for two distinct types of sacrifice: thanksgiving and guilt. The first was natural to our creaturely condition: tribute offering brought to the Great King. In Romans 1, Paul says that the first evidence of our fall in Adam was that we were no longer thankful. After the fall, something else was needed: a guilt offering, a sacrifice to take away sins.

It's amazing how this idea of falling short and the gods being angry with us permeates the world's religions. That's why they threw kids into volcanoes as they offered an annual sacrifice of a person, and created elaborate schemes to appease the gods or the forces of nature. "If we just do x, then god or the gods will do y." This law-logic is evident even in Christianity; it's our natural religion, our default setting.

Yet the good news is that God provides the sacrifice for guilt. After the fall in Genesis 3, God clothed Adam and Eve with sacrificial skins, pointing to the Lamb of God who takes away the sin of the world. God wasn't bound in any way to do this. It's a sheer act of free mercy on his part. The whole sacrificial system of the Old Testament pointed forward to the moment when God the Son, in our flesh, would bear the curse for our sin and bring an end to all sacrifices.

Now we live in a grace economy, not a debt economy. At last we are free to be thankful, to offer ourselves as "living sacrifices" of praise rather than dead sacrifices of guilt. We're on the receiving end of everything. We're not building a kingdom, but receiving one. We're not appeasing God, but receiving his gift of righteousness in his Son.

As recipient of this covenantal exchange between the Father and the incarnate Son, the church lives in an economy of gratitude rather than either sacrifice or as an extension of Christ's atoning work. *We are passive receivers of the gift of salvation, but we are thereby rendered active worshipers in a life of thanksgiving that is exhibited chiefly in loving service to our neighbors.*

Especially when we gather for corporate worship, we are reminded again that beneath all of the contracts we have conducted throughout the week, reality is fundamentally ordered by God's covenantal faithfulness. God speaks and we respond with thanksgiving. Here the logic of the market (debt) is disrupted by the doxological logic of grace (gift).

Christ is both the fully satisfying thank offering (a life well-pleasing to God on our behalf) and guilt offering (substitute for our sins). Notice especially the two crucial points made in 2 Corinthians 1:19–20: "For the Son of God, Jesus Christ, whom we proclaimed among you ... was not Yes and No, but in him it is always Yes. For all the promises of God find their Yes in him. That is why it is through him that we utter our Amen to God for his glory." By fulfilling our debts, he makes our lives thank offerings to God. He puts a new economy in its place, so that "through him" we can "say Amen to God for his glory." The Gift has been given; therefore, we are free to give: thanks to God, and our good works to our neighbor.

Until people are persuaded that God is the fountain of all of our good, Calvin insists, "they will never devote themselves wholly, truly, and sincerely to him."[98] Grace inspires gratitude. "There is ... an exact parallel in this respect between piety and faith," notes Calvin scholar Brian Gerrish. Only because of the forgiveness of sins that comes from Christ can the uneasy conscience ever be assured that God is indeed good and the source of all good.[99]

From God alone, therefore, all good and perfect gifts come to the world and are then distributed by us for the feast. The church is the place where sinners are receivers, yet it is also the people who are scattered to fulfill their common callings. In the latter, the church has no dominion. It cannot command the covenant community to embrace particular political ideologies, policies, parties, or politicians. It can only witness to the kingdom of grace, not inaugurate the kingdom of glory. Hence, Calvin as well as Luther refers to "two kingdoms" that must be kept distinct in the present age, although the believer participates in both.[100]

Gustav Wingren nicely summarizes Luther's concern with the neighbor as the recipient of the believer's good works. Instead of living in monasteries, committing their lives in service to themselves and their own salvation, or living in castles, commanding the world to mirror the kingdom of Christ, Luther argues, believers should love and serve their neighbors through their vocations in the world, where their neighbors need them.[101] "God does not need our good works, but our neighbor does."[102] When we offer our works to God, we simultaneously "attempt to depose Christ from his throne" and neglect our neighbor, since these works "have clearly been done, not for the sake of [our] neighbor, but to parade before God."[103] God descends to serve humanity through our vocations, so instead of seeing good works as our works for God, they are now to be seen as God's work for our neighbor, which God performs through us. That is why both orders are upset when we seek to present good works to God as if he needed them. In contrast, when we are overwhelmed by the superabundance of God's gracious gift, we express our gratitude in horizontal works of love and service to the neighbor.

This view of vocation had numerous implications for social life. "In his *Treatise on Christian Liberty*, the main thought is that a Christian lives in Christ through faith and in his neighbor through love."[104]

> In faith, which accepts the gift, man finds that it is not only "heaven that is pure with its stars, where Christ reigns in his work," but the earth too is clean "with its trees and its grass, where we are at home with all that is ours." There is nothing more delightful and

lovable on earth than one's neighbor. Love does not think about doing works, it finds joy in people; and when something good is done for others, that does not appear to love as works but simply as gifts which flow naturally from love.[105]

Under the law, in Adam, one is trapped in the cycle of sin and death, resentment and despair, self-righteousness and self-condemnation. Yet under grace, in Christ, one is not only justified apart from the law but is able for the first time to respond to that law of love that calls from the deepest recesses of our being as covenantally constituted creatures. It is not the law itself that changes, but our relation to it, that makes all the difference.

In an economy of grace, there is enough to go around. The Father's love and generosity are not scarce. His table is brimming with luxurious fare. That is why we invite those who cannot repay us. After all, it is not our table, but his. It is Christ who speaks to us today in the words of the prophet:

Come, everyone who thirsts,
    come to the waters;
and he who has no money,
    come, buy and eat!
Come, buy wine and milk
    without money and without price.
Why do you spend your money for that which is not bread,
    and your labor for that which does not satisfy?
Listen diligently to me, and eat what is good,
    and delight yourselves in rich food. (Isa 55:1–2)

God's liberal hand is open to us and opens us up to the others seated with us. We begin to delight not only in God but in our neighbor. We're no longer *modern masters*, or *postmodern tourists*, but *forgiven pilgrims* on our way to the city God has built, as he spreads a table in the wilderness for us on our way.

Just as the gospel directs us outside of ourselves to the divine stranger who meets us in peace and reconciliation, it frees us for an extroverted piety that is no longer obsessed with either self-condemnation or self-justification. It enables us to concentrate not on the inward process of infused habits and our own moral progress, but to turn our attention outward to the fellow strangers all around us. The gospel makes us extrospective, turning our gaze upward to God in faith and outward to our neighbor in love. This is true freedom—freedom from sin's guilt and tyranny, so that we can actually love people as gifts instead of debts.

Entering God's Rest

The Lord's Day is not another treadmill, but a day of resting from our works as we bask in his marvelous provision for our salvation and temporal needs (Heb 4:1–5). After all, "the earth is the LORD's and the fullness thereof" (Ps 24:1). On this holy day, we rest in God's care for our temporal welfare. But even more than that, we rest in him alone for everlasting life. It is the opportunity to receive a kingdom rather than to build one; to be beneficiaries rather than benefactors; to be heirs rather than employees; to be on the receiving end once again of "the Son of Man [who] came not to be served but to serve, and to give his life as a ransom for many" (Matt 20:28). We can be still and know that Yahweh is God (Ps 46:10).

This rest is not a cessation from all activity, however. It's joining our Lord in his conquest over death and hell, receiving and dispensing the spoils of his victory. It's opening the windows to the beams radiating from the age to come, where Christ reigns in grace, anticipating together that day when he returns to reign in glory. Filled with the intensity of such sovereign grace, the Lord's Day becomes a beachhead for the transformation of our whole lives, so that every day is warmed by its light.

"God rested on the seventh day from all his works" (Heb 4:4). Yet Israel, like Adam, failed the test and therefore forfeited the Sabbath rest. As Paul says in Romans 10, ironically, Israel pursued it by works but didn't attain it, while those who didn't pursue it by works but received it by faith did attain it. Unlike all of the high priests of the old covenant, "we have a great high priest who has passed through the heavens, Jesus, the Son of God" (4:14). Taking his throne at the

Father's right hand, he has claimed it as our throne together with him in everlasting glory. "Let us then with confidence draw near to the throne of grace, that we may receive mercy and find grace to help in time of need" (4:16).

So again there is another "today": the space in history to enter the everlasting Sabbath day with God by resting from our works because Christ has fulfilled all of our daily labors on our behalf. He calls us not to toil for that rest by our guarding, subduing, and keeping, but simply to enter *his* rest through faith behind the conquering King.

Unstoppable?

"You are all going to die." It's not the message that college grads are used to hearing, which may be why the 2012 commencement speech by screenwriter Joss Whedon created so much media buzz. In our youth culture, even mature adults are encouraged to recover their inner teenager. "I may be old, but I'll never grow up," I read just yesterday on a vanity plate.

But there is no denying that it's harder to keep up with expectations. The most taboo topic in our society is death. At least in California, people don't die; they just "pass away" — or better yet, live on in their legacy and the memories they leave behind. Make no mistake about it: death stalks us and eventually stops us in our tracks. Wisdom calls us to use this fact as a trigger to reorient us to the things that really matter. As it turns out, they're the everyday things.

The truth is that each of us is stoppable. In fact, we all stop. Our heart stops beating, we stop moving, and we stop breathing. As Whedon pointed out in his commencement address, we even start winding down just as our ambitions are all wound up.

The Stoic in all of us imagines that we are independent of God and each other, until we're not. In *The Little Way of Ruth Leming*, Rod Dreher reflects:

> Contemporary culture encourages us to make islands of ourselves
> for the sake of self-fulfillment, of career advancement, of entertainment, of diversion, and all the demands of the sovereign self. When

suffering and death come for you—and it will—you want to be in a place where you know, and are known. You want—no, you need—to be able to say, as Mike did, "We're leaning, but we're leaning on each other."[106]

Dreher's sister, Ruth, never left the small Louisiana town where they were raised, but lived an ordinary life of loving service in her community. When she contracted cancer, he moved back home, leaving the dazzling heights of New York journalism. A friend tells him, " 'Everything I've done has been for career advancement. Go for the money, the good jobs. And we have done well. But we are alone in the world,' he said. 'Almost everybody I know is like that. My family is all over the country. My kids only call if they want something ... when we get old, our kids can't move back to take care of us if they wanted to because we all go off to some golf resort to retire. This is the world we have made for ourselves. I envy you that you can escape it.' "[107] Dreher adds:

> Never would I have imagined that I would spend the morning of my little sister's forty-third birthday in the graveyard, watching workmen heave her tombstone into place. But nobody ever thinks about these things when they're young. Nobody thinks about limits, and how much we need each other. But if you live long enough, you see suffering. It comes close to you. It shatters the illusion, so dear to us, of self-sufficiency, of autonomy, of control. Look, a wife and mother, a good woman in the prime of her life, dying from cancer. It doesn't just happen to other people. It happens to your family. What do you do then?[108]

"So teach us to number our days that we may get a heart of wisdom" (Ps 90:12). When we do that, we shrink a little bit, but God and his world grow much larger. And whenever that happens, we are ready to make the most of the ordinary.

Exercise

1. How are women especially, even from childhood, given expectations that can be overwhelming, confusing, and impossible?

2. Do you tend sometimes to treat people as projects? Why do we do this and how should we view them?

3. What are the two different types of sacrifice in the Old Testament? How does Christ fulfill both and what does that mean for our lives today?

4. Do you draw strength for your active life of faith from an ultimate place of resting in Christ? What are the challenges to this in our daily lives?

5. Consider/discuss the youth-dominated emphasis on being "unstoppable." How does our outlook change as we grow older? (This one is especially good to discuss in a group with varying ages.)

CHAPTER 11

after ordinary: anticipating the revolution

Everyone is driven in the present by an expectation of the future. According to the spirit of our age, we came from nowhere and are going to nowhere, but in between we can make something of ourselves.

Christians are driven by a different story. Our origins are extraordinarily noble, but we rebelled against this dependent glory. Not content to be the moon, reflecting the sun's glory, we demanded to be the sun itself. And yet, some extraordinary events have occurred in history to redeem us—and our history—from sin and death. And the destiny on which we have set our hopes is anything but ordinary. It is nothing less than "the resurrection of the body and life everlasting." One day, there will be no distinction between heaven and earth. Faith will give way to sight. Then we won't live on promises anymore. There won't be an ordinary day. The Next Big Thing is Christ's return. Until then, we live in hope that changes our ordinary lives here and now.

Christ has already secured this glorious destiny for us as the "firstfruits," but everything in our own daily experience seems to count against it. Our bodies decay, we lose our memory, and we seem to be falling apart just when we wanted to save the world. Apart from the surprising announcement of the gospel, we would vacillate between utopianism and nihilism. From everything we see around us and in our own lives, this gospel seems too good to be true.

Not As Good As It Gets

The life we're living right now prepares for everything after the resurrection of the dead. This event will not inaugurate the end of time, but the end of time as measured by the law of sin and death. It will not be the end of this world, but its rebirth. In Scripture, the Sabbath was to time what the Holy Land, with the temple at its heart, was to space. They were a preview, brief intimations, of coming attractions. In the kingdom that Christ inaugurated and will consummate at his return, every day will be the everlasting Sabbath and the whole earth—in fact, the whole cosmos—will be his sanctuary.

Measured against that sort of radical event, our lives seem exceedingly brief. Yet the age to come is not sealed off from our lives here and now. Instead, the picture we get dimly in the prophets and more clearly in the New Testament is that the age to come is already penetrating into this present evil age by the powerful energy of the Holy Spirit.

Working through the ordinary means of grace, the Spirit not only gives us good things. He is himself the gift of the Father and the Son. In many premodern societies, a person might surrender something valuable, like a cloak, to secure a loan. In extreme cases, one might offer a family member as a pledge or deposit until the full loan was repaid. In Scripture, however, we are told that God himself has been given by God as the deposit. The Father and the Son have given the Holy Spirit, "who is the guarantee of our inheritance until we acquire possession of it, to the praise of his glory" (Eph 1:14).

It is the Holy Spirit who renovates and who tends the garden—both within us and between us and the other branches—ensuring that we bear the fruit of the Spirit: patience, love, burden-bearing, self-control, and other attributes appropriate to the "already-not yet" tension of our lives here and now.

It would be easier to live in an "either-or" world. We could be "dead in the trespasses and sins," ignoring God's claims and his saving work on our behalf. Or we could be glorified, perfected in body and soul, here and now. But both of these are delusions, if we are in Christ. There are no first-class Christians who have attained victory over all known sin and the curse that is common to humanity since the fall. Nor are there carnal Christians who are forgiven but devoid of the Spirit and his sanctifying power.

There are two kinds of prosperity gospels. One promises personal health, wealth, and happiness. Another promises social transformation. In both versions, the results are up to us. We bring God's kingdom to earth, either to ourselves or to society, by following certain spiritual laws or moral and political agendas. Both forget that salvation comes from above, as a gift of God. Both forget that because we are baptized into Christ, the pattern of our lives is suffering leading to glory in that cataclysmic revolution that Christ will bring when he returns. Both miss the point that our lives and the world as they are now are not as good as it gets. We do not have our best life or world now.

However, the opposite danger is to ignore the good news that the new creation has already begun. Christ has already inaugurated his kingdom, even though he has not yet consummated it. If we wall off this coming kingdom as entirely future, we may easily confuse "ordinary" with this present age that is fading away.

The difficult place to stand is at that precarious intersection of this present age, which is captive to sin and death, and the age to come, which is the fruit of Christ's victory that the Spirit is planting, tending, and spreading in our hearts and in our world through the gospel. The garden is growing, but like a bright patch weather-beaten by the conflict between these two ages. The hot winds blow hard against us, but the Spirit's cool breeze of grace keeps the garden blossoming and spreading across the desert.

The Next Big Thing — No, the Real One

"Behold, I am making all things new!" (Rev 21:5). There is something in the revolutionary impulse that is borrowed from the gospel. The church indeed proclaims with the prophets and the apostles that our Lord Jesus Christ has inaugurated a kingdom that will, at its consummation, assimilate all powers and worldly regimes to itself. This proclamation is more radical concerning the guilt and misery of the human race than any pessimist and more joyful in the prospect of a completely transformed cosmos than the most cheerful optimist. Furthermore, it announces the complete forgiveness of sins and justification. The good news does not even terminate in regenerated individuals with God's peace in their hearts. These marvelous truths give us confidence that in spite of how things look, God's promise stands firm even now, while you and I still fall short of the glory of God. Yet the ultimate benefit of our salvation is that we will be like God, and that the whole creation will be renewed by the energies of the Spirit.

It is as if the whole world were crying out for the liberation Paul describes in Romans 8. Even the atheistic revolutionary feels the need to steal roses from the Christian garden to dignify his utopian vision. In fact, the modern dogma of progress is little more than a secularized version of the biblical promise of a redeemed world without deprivation, injustice, war, and strife.

As I have argued in an earlier chapter, the longing for the Next Big Thing has often been bound up with a view of salvation centering on a radical conversion experience and a view of the Christian life as punctuated by these radical moments. There is certainly a truth here as well. Who can dispute the radical character of a new birth that makes those spiritually dead alive in Christ?

The problem is not that we acknowledge with Scripture the radical character of salvation or the radical newness of the world in the age to come, but that we expect the consummation to come too soon. The passive believer has forgotten the newness that the Spirit has already brought into this world through the word of Christ. He or she may believe that things will be new in the future, when Christ returns. But instead of experiencing life now as the firstfruits of that consummation, he or she seems to view this life as relatively unchanged and untouched by God's advent in Jesus Christ. The activist saint, however, may forget that The Next Big Thing in God's timetable is the return of Christ. Only his return can bring about that absolute division in history between the time of death and the time of everlasting life.

The difficult but necessary location of Christian existence for now is that paradoxical era of the "already and not-yet." The Next Big Thing is not another Pentecost or another apostle or another political or social cause. It is Christ's return. In demanding an immediate satisfaction of our heart's longing, we replace this event with manufactured spectacles. Ironically, the most faithful Christian life is one that embraces a pilgrimage rather than a conquest. The ordinary life—sustainable discipleship and disciple-making—is the order of the day, as we live each moment in eager expectation of The Next Big Thing on God's schedule.

If You Knew Jesus Were Returning Tomorrow

What if you knew that Jesus would return tomorrow morning? That question was asked often in church as I was growing up. In case we didn't have a ready answer, we were usually told what we *should* be found doing. The question was meant to light the fire underneath us for extraordinary undertakings. Who would want to be found grocery shopping or driving home from work? However, wiser Christians remind us that being found at our daily callings, glorifying and enjoying God in ordinary ways, is a better answer. Taking in the April scent and clucking chickens from his window, Luther is reported to have said, "Even if I knew the world was going to end tomorrow, I would still plant an apple tree today."

Even if this is one of the many spurious Luther quotes, it still expresses a biblical wisdom he often shared.[109] After all, the apostle Paul answered this question directly in 1 Thessalonians 4. As the day of the Lord approaches, he says, believers are "to aspire to live quietly, and to mind [their] own affairs, and to work with [their] hands" (4:11). It doesn't sound very world-transforming. Yet it is precisely in the habits that make up a life like this that believers live "properly before outsiders and [are] dependent on no one" (v 12).

As we have seen, each of us is a branch of the Vine, as well as a worker in the vineyard. Paul spoke of this especially in reference to himself and other ministers of the Word. Some plant, some water, but it is the Lord who makes it grow. Isn't that liberating?

What did you do for the kingdom today? How did you impact the world for Christ? Our tendency might be to hesitate at that point, trying desperately to recall something worth reporting. Yet every day, in all sorts of ways we're not even aware of, the kingdom is growing and our neighbors are being served. There may be a quiet reference in the coffee room that provokes a coworker weeks later to ask a question about life and death, maybe even addressing it not to you but to another believer. You made lunch for the kids and got them to school on time. You worked well with your hands to supply neighbors with what they need and — oh, again, "I will build my church, and the gates of hell shall not prevail against it" (Matt 16:18). Keep on point. Don't lose the focus. Jesus has bound Satan (Mark 3:27; Luke 10:17). Now we are free to do the little things that matter, without anxiety about how it all turns out in the end. "In the world you will have tribulation. But take heart; I have overcome the world" (John 16:33).

Last Call: Dying as a Vocation

Wise Christians in the past thought of life as in some deep sense a preparation for death. It's replete in the Puritan literature, with popular books on "dying well." We were not created for this death. It is unnatural to us, despite the upbeat way we trivialize it — mainly out of fear. Death cannot have a purpose, any transcendent meaning, according to many of our neighbors, because if it did, that might lead us to wonder if it was some sort of divine judgment on us. Our culture is pathologically committed to postponing and even denying the reality of death, because it does not know about the justification of the ungodly that removes the sting and the resurrection that gives our lives a happy beginning, not ending, beyond anything we've ever known. So instead of funerals, we have "celebrations of life," with upbeat memories of the departed.

Because of the gospel, believers are free to embrace their final cross, death, as a calling from God. After years of various callings as children, parents, neighbors, employers and employees, and so forth, our last one is to face death not with Stoic self-confidence but with the assurance that it is indeed "the last enemy" and it won't have the last word (1 Cor 15:26). God calls us first and foremost to cast ourselves into his care, safe in the mediation of his Son and sustained by his Spirit. From this confidence, he calls us to witness to our family, neighbors, and friends that we are not "passing on," but dying. And yet our hope ultimately is to be raised in the glorious likeness of Jesus Christ.

Living each day in the light of this "last enemy" and the assurance of Christ's ultimate victory over it, we weep but do not lose heart as we face suffering in milder forms. The apostle Paul could pursue the course that would lead ultimately to his martyrdom not out of vain ambition, but on behalf of Christ and in service to others. "Therefore, having this ministry by the mercy of God, we do not lose heart. But we have renounced disgraceful, underhanded ways. We refuse to practice cunning or to tamper with God's word" (2 Cor 4:1–2a). This is in sharp contrast with the "super-apostles." They drew crowds because of their natural gifts.

> But we have this treasure in jars of clay, to show that the surpassing power belongs to God and not to us. We are afflicted in every way, but not crushed; perplexed, but not driven to despair; persecuted, but not forsaken, struck down, but not destroyed; always carrying in the body the death of Jesus, so that the life of Jesus may also be manifested in our bodies.... So death is at work in us, but life in you. (2 Cor 4:7–10, 12)

A theology of glory looks at the outward appearance of things, but the theology of the cross is riveted to the promise that is heard: "So we do not lose heart. Though our outer self is wasting away, our inner self is being renewed day by day. For this slight momentary affliction is preparing for us an eternal weight of glory beyond all comparison, as we look not to the things that are seen but to the things that are unseen" (4:16–18).

The contrast between seen and unseen is not Plato's lower and upper worlds. It is not as if the visible world we know is a mere shadow compared with the invisible realm of pure spirit. Instead of two worlds, the apostles have in mind two ages: this world in its present form, under the reign of sin and death, and this world in its redeemed and resurrected form when Christ returns. Even now, the rays of the age to come are piercing this present age. As Paul teaches above, the final resurrection has already begun with Jesus as its firstfruits, along with the regeneration of the inner self. What we see and can measure visibly counts against this new creation, but we live by the promise.

Already the wall separating Gentiles from Jews, symbolized by the temple's outer court of the Gentiles and the inner court, has been torn down in Christ. In Christ, we enter not only the Holy Place, but the Most Holy Place, where not even Jews could enter except representatively in the high priest. As we learn from John's vision in Revelation, even the boundary between heaven and earth will disappear. God's throne room will no longer be invisible to us, nor even visible merely in one earthly capitol, but it will be in the middle of us. His glory will fill the earth and renew it day by day.

Heaven on earth at last. It's not a dream. It has been secured already by Christ's victory over sin and death. Yet for now it is a promise, with an advance on our final treasure being given in regular installments.

The life that we live now by the Spirit is therefore already a down payment or security deposit on the blessings of the age to come. We can live with the ordinary world, with its common curse and common grace, with our ordinary growth in Christ through the ordinary means of grace, and with our ordinary callings in the family, the church, and the world. We can be content in the ups and downs, because we have every spiritual blessing in Christ and we share it with our fellow saints in the exchange of gifts.

Now we can see more clearly that the vices that have warped us are corruptions of original gifts. We were made to hunger and thirst for glory, but we wanted it apart from God—on our own terms. Yet in Christ we will be glorified far beyond the condition of Adam and Eve in the garden. All of our desires—and others of which we weren't even explicitly aware—will be satisfied beyond our wildest imagining.

It is precisely because of this extraordinary hope, therefore, that we can embrace the ordinary lives God gives us here and now.

For I consider that the sufferings of this present time are not worth comparing with the glory that is to be revealed to us. For the creation waits with eager longing for the revealing of the sons of God. For the creation was subjected to futility, not willingly, but because of him who subjected it, in hope that the creation itself will be set free from its bondage to corruption and obtain the freedom of the glory of the children of God. For we know that the whole creation has been groaning together in the pains of childbirth until now. And not only the creation, but we ourselves, who have the firstfruits of the Spirit, groan inwardly as we wait eagerly for adoption as sons, the redemption of our bodies. For in this hope we were saved. Now hope that is seen is not hope. For who hopes for what he sees? But if we hope for what we do not see, we wait for it with patience. (Rom 8:18–25)

That's enough to make even our ordinary lives a foretaste of the extraordinary revolution that is on its way.

Exercise

1. How does the extraordinary hope of final redemption shed new light on our ordinary lives here and now?
2. We live as Christians in the tension between the "already" and the "not yet." What does this mean? Is it practically relevant for our daily lives?
3. What would you do if you knew that Jesus was coming back today? Why?
4. Is dying a vocation? If so, how does that reorient our thinking about living each day?

notes

1. See www.theonion.com/articles/unambitious-loser-with-happy-fulfilling-life-still,33233/ (accessed 7/30/2013).

2. Heather Havrilesky, "All Hail Lord Business!" *The New York Times Magazine* (March 2, 2014), 46–47.

3. Tish Harrison Warren, "Courage in the Ordinary," written Wednesday, April 3, 2013, at http://thewell.intervarsity.org/blog/courage-ordinary (accessed February 26, 2014).

4. Rod Dreher, "Everydayness," Nov. 14, 2012 at www.theamericanconservative.com/dreher/everydayness-wallace-stevens/ (accessed July 7, 2013).

5. www.christianitytoday.com/ct/2007/march/7.53.html (accessed December 1, 2013).

6. My colleague, Pastor Kim Riddlebarger, has written a series of insightful reflections on Orange County's series of Christian empires at http://kimriddlebarger.squarespace.com/the-latest-post/2013/12/18/the-changing-religious-climate-of-orange-county-revisited-an.html (accessed November 2, 2013).

7. Jim Hinch, "Where Are the People," *The American Scholar*, at http://theamericanscholar.org/where-are-the-people/#.UrSVQ2yA1dg (accessed December 1, 2013).

8. Tish Harrison Warren, "Courage in the Ordinary." The author's insights may also be heard in an

interview I conducted with her at www.whitehorseinn.org/
blog/2013/09/01/whi–1169-courage-in-the-ordinary/.

9. Collin Hansen, *Young, Restless and Reformed: A Journalist's Journey with the New Calvinists* (Wheaton, IL: Crossway, 2008).

10. See James K. A. Smith, *Letters to a Young Calvinist: An Invitation to the Reformed Tradition* (Grand Rapids: Brazos, 2010).

11. Thomas J. Peters and Nancy K. Austin, *A Passion for Excellence: The Leadership Difference* (New York: Warner, 1985), xvii.

12. Quoted in Gustav Wingren, *Luther on Vocation* (trans. Carl C. Rasmussen; Evansville, IN: Ballast, 1994), 10.

13. Herman Selderhuis, *Calvin's Theology of the Psalms*, 235.

14. The Heidelberg Catechism, Q & A 1, from the Christian Reformed Church translation: www.crcna.org/welcome/beliefs/confessions/heidelberg-catechism.

15. Ibid., Q & A 114.

16. Ibid., Q & A 115.

17. See www.christianitytoday.com/ct/2012/june/when-are-we-going-to-grow-up.html.

18. Ibid. See also Thomas E. Bergler, *The Juvenilization of American Christianity* (Grand Rapids: Eerdmans, 2012).

19. Joe Queenan, *Balsamic Dreams: A Short but Self-Important History of the Baby Boomer Generation* (New York: Henry Hold, 2001), 23.

20. Ibid., 24.

21. Friedrich Nietzsche, *The Antichrist* §2.

22. C. S. Lewis, *The Weight of Glory* (new ed.; New York: HarperOne, 2009), 26.

23. "William Bennett Quotes." http://thinkexist.com/quotes/William–Bennett/ (accessed March 18, 2014).

24. David Brooks, *Bobos in Paradise: The New Upper Class and How They Got There* (New York: Simon and Schuster, 2001).

25. (New York: Atria, 2007).

26. Dr. Keith Ablow, "We Are Raising a Generation of Deluded Narcissists" (FoxNews.com, January 8, 2013). See also the White Horse Inn interview with Jean Twenge at www.whitehorseinn.org/blog/2012/06/24/whi-1107-the-narcissism-epidemic/.

27. John Culkin, "A Schoolman's Guide to Marshal McLughan," *Saturday Review*, March 18, 1967.

28. Nicholas Carr, *The Shallows: How the Internet Is Changing Our Brains* (New York: Norton, 2011).

29. (New York: Basic Books, 2011).

30. Joseph Heath and Andrew Potter, *A Nation of Rebels: Why Counterculture Became Consumer Culture* (New York: Harper Business, 2004).

31. C. S. Lewis, *The Screwtape Letters* (New York: Macmillan, 1945), chap 25.

32. Ibid., 118.

33. G. K. Chesterton, *Illustrated London News* (March 19, 1924).

34. Abraham Kuyper, *Principles of Sacred Theology* (trans. J. Vriend; Grand Rapids: Baker Academic, 1980), 574–75.

35. Quoted from Miroslav Volf, *After Our Likeness* (Grand Rapids: Eerdmans, 1993), 161–62.

36. Ian Murray, *Revival and Revivalism: The Making and Marring of American Evangelicalism, 1750–1850* (Edinburgh: Banner of Truth, 1994). I find his distinction between revival and revivalism persuasive and helpful. Nevertheless, the open question is whether emphasizing the former has not also undermined the ordinary ministry.

37. Ironically, Finney held to an *ex opere operato* view of his own new measures that he would never allow to baptism and the Supper. As for the Pelagian charge, Finney's *Systematic*

Theology (Minneapolis: Bethany, 1976) explicitly denies original sin and insists that the power of regeneration lies in the sinner's own hands, rejects any substitutionary notion of Christ's atonement in favor of the moral influence and moral government theories, and regards the doctrine of justification by an alien righteousness as "impossible and absurd." In fact, Roger Olson, in his defense of Arminianism, sees Finney's theology as well beyond the Arminian pale (*Arminian Theology* [Downers Grove, IL: InterVarsity Press, 2006], 27). Thus, it is all the more remarkable that Finney occupies such a distinguished place among evangelicals, as the tribute to him in the Billy Graham Center (at Wheaton, Illinois) illustrates. It is little wonder that American religion struck Bonhoeffer as "Protestantism without the Reformation."

38. Charles G. Finney, *Revivals of Religion* (Old Tappan, NJ: Revell, n.d.), 321.

39. Quoted in Michael Pasquarello III, *Christian Preaching: A Trinitarian Theology of Proclamation* (Grand Rapids: Baker Academic, 2007), 24.

40. Charles Finney, *Lectures on Revival* (2nd ed.; New York: Leavitt, Lord, 1835), 184–204. "Law, rewards, and punishments—these things and such as these are the very heart and soul of moral suasion.... My brethren, if ecclesiastical bodies, colleges, and seminaries will only go forward—who will not bid them God speed? But if they will not go forward—if we hear nothing from them but complaint, denunciation, and rebuke in respect to almost every branch of reform, what can be done?"

41. John Williamson Nevin, *The Anxious Bench* (London: Taylor & Francis, 1987), 2–5.

42. See Keith J. Hardman, *Charles Grandison Finney: Revivalist and Reformer* (Grand Rapids, Baker, 1990), 380–94.

43. See, e.g., Whitney R. Cross, *The Burned-Over District: The Social and Intellectual History of Enthusiastic Religion in*

Western New York, 1800–1850 (Ithaca, NY: Cornell University Press, 1982).

44. Garry Wills, *Head and Heart: American Christianities* (New York: Penguin, 2007), 294.

45. Ibid., 302.

46. See the previous chapter, p. 54.

47. Henri de Lubac, *A Brief Catechesis on Nature & Grace* (trans. Brother Richard Arnandez; San Francisco: Ignatius, 1984), 56–58.

48. Dave Harvey, *Rescuing Ambition* (Wheaton. IL: Crossway, 2010), 14–15. Harvey makes a great case for rescuing ambition and I don't disagree at all in substance. Yet I still think it's worth following its transformation from vice to virtue and suggest that instead of rescuing it, we should replace it with words like "drive" or "passion."

49. *Metamorphoses* Book 8, ll. 78–94; see http://readytogoe-books.com/classics/Ovid-icarus.htm.

50. William Casey King, *Ambition, A History: From Vice to Virtue* (New Haven, CT: Yale University Press, 2013).

51. Ibid., 101.

52. John Donne, "Anatomy of the World," see http://www.poetryfoundation.org/poem/173348.

53. Quoted in King, *Ambition*, 82.

54. Ibid., 91.

55. This hymn was written in 1848. See www.cyberhymnal.org/htm/a/l/allthing.htm.

56. King, *Ambition*, 94–118.

57. Ibid., 93.

58. www.theatlantic.com/video/archive/2013/04/millennials-vs-earlier-generations-a-scorecard/275049/.

59. Friedrich Nietzche, *Twilight of the Idols* in *The Portable*

Nietzsche (trans. Walter Kaufmann; New York: Penguin, 1976), 502.

60. Nietzsche, *The Will to Power* (ed. Walter Kaufmann; trans. Walter Kaufmann and R. J. Hollingdale; New York: Random House, 1967), 101.

61. A. W. Tozer, *Man: The Dwelling Place of God* (Camp Hill, PA: Wingspread, 2008), 16–17.

62. For a provocative analysis of this point, see James K. A. Smith, *Desiring the Kingdom: Worship, Worldview, and Cultural Formation* (Grand Rapids: Baker Academic, 2009).

63. Note in a similar vein, in Matt 7:22, those on the outside point to all of the mighty works they supposedly did in Jesus' name: prophesying, casting out demons, and performing mighty works.

64. Jerome, "Letter CXLVI (To Evangelus)," in *Library of Nicene and Post-Nicene Fathers* (ed. Phillip Schaff; Grand Rapids: Eerdmans, 1988), 288–89; Ambrose, *Commentary on Ephesians* 4.2, cited in Samuel Miller, "Presbyterianism: The Apostolic Constitution," in *Paradigms in Polity* (ed. David W. Hall and Joseph H. Hall; Grand Rapids: Eerdmans, 1994), 57–58.

65. Over several pages Jerome cites examples from Acts and the Epistles to demonstrate that presbyter and bishop were one and the same office, "but gradually, as the seed beds of dissensions were eradicated, all solicitude was conferred on one man ... more by custom than by the truth of the Lord's arrangement." *St. Jerome's Commentaries on Galatians, Titus, and Philemon* (trans. Thomas P. Scheck; Notre Dame: University of Notre Dame Press, 2010), 288–90.

66. Gregory I, *Letters* in *Leo the Great, Gregory the Great*. In *Nicene and Post-Nicene Fathers*, vol. 12, second series (trans. Henry Wace, ed. Philip Schaff; various publishers), i.75–76; ii.170, 171, 179, 166, 169, 222, 225.

67. Second Helvetic Confession, ch. 1.

68. Geoff Surratt, Greg Ligon, and Warren Bird, *The Multi-Site Church Revolution: Being One Church in Many Locations* (Grand Rapids: Zondervan, 2006), 18.

69. See footnote 65.

70. Surratt, Ligon, and Bird, *The Multi-Site Church Revolution*, 18.

71. From Martin Luther's hymn, "A Mighty Fortress Is Our God."

72. Tim Kasser, *The High Price of Materialism* (Cambridge, MA: MIT Press, 2002), 3.

73. Ibid., 12.

74. Adam Smith, *An Inquiry in to Nature and Causes of the Wealth of Nations* (Glasgow edition of the works and correspondence of Adam Smith; ed. R. H. Campbell and A. S. Skinner; Oxford: Clarendon, 1976), 2:456.

75. Kasser, *The High Price of Materialism*, 49.

76. Ibid., 50.

77. Ibid., 12.

78. Ibid., 67.

79. Ibid., 70.

80. Ibid., 67.

81. John Calvin, *Institutes of the Christian Religion* (ed. John T. McNeill; trans. Ford Lewis Battles; Philadelphia: Westminster, 1960), 2.2.15.

82. Ibid.

83. Ibid., 4.20.8, 14.

84. Luther, "Sermon on the Commemoration of Bridget of Sweden," quoted in H. D. M. Spence and Joseph S. Excell, eds., *The Pulpit Commentary* (Grand Rapids: Eerdmans, 1950), 20:323.

85. See James D. Hunter, *To Change the World* (Oxford: Oxford University Press, 2010).

86. www.challies.com/music-movies/another-switchfoot-concert (retrieved December 16, 2013).

87. George Eliot, *Middlemarch* (London: Penguin, 1994), 838.

88. J. I. Packer and Gary A. Parrett, *Grounded in the Gospel: Building Believers the Old-Fashioned Way* (Grand Rapids: Baker, 2010), 96.

89. Carl Trueman, "On Pastoral Succession," at www.reformation21.org/blog/2011/06/on-pastoral-succession.php (accessed March 18, 2014).

90. Kasser, *The High Price of Materialism*, 91.

91. Larry Alex Taunton, "Listening to Youth Atheists: Lessons for a Stronger Christianity," *The Atlantic* (June 6, 2013), available at www.theatlantic.com/national/archive/2013/06/listening-to-young-atheists-lessons-for-a-stronger-christianity/276584/ (accessed March 10, 2014).

92. Ivy Beckwith, *Formational Children's Ministry: Shaping Children Using Story, Ritual, and Relationship* (Grand Rapids: Baker, 2010), 98.

93. Kenda Creasy Dean, *Almost Christian: What the Faith of Our Teenagers Is Telling the American Church* (Oxford: Oxford University Press, 2010), 3.

94. Kate Murphy, "Is Youth Ministry Killing the Church?" at www.christiancentury.org/blogs/archive/2010–02/youth-ministry-killing-church (accessed March 10, 2014).

95. See Packer and Parrett, *Grounded in the Gospel*.

96. See Brian Cosby, *Giving Up Gimmicks: Recovering Youth Ministry from an Entertainment Culture* (Phillipsburg, NJ: Presbyterian & Reformed, 2012).

97. www.whitehorseinn.org/blog/page/2/#sthash.k4HPTftD.dpuf.

98. John Calvin, *Institutes*, 1.2.2.

99. Ibid., 3.3.19.

100. Ibid., 4.20.1–3.

101. Gustav Wingren, *Luther on Vocation* (trans. Carl C. Rasmussen; Evansville, IN: Ballast, 1994; reprinted from Augsburg-Fortress edition), 2.

102. Ibid., 10.

103. Ibid., 13, 31.

104. Ibid., 42.

105. Ibid., 43.

106. Rod Dreher, *The Little Way of Ruth Leming: A Southern Girl, a Small Town, and the Secret of a Good Life* (New York: Grand Central, 2013), 209.

107. Ibid., 216.

108. Ibid., 267.

109. See the excellent treatment by Gene Edward Veith, *God At Work: Finding Your Christian Vocation in All of Life* (Wheaton, IL: Crossway, 2002).

A Place for Weakness

Preparing Yourself for Suffering

Michael S. Horton

In a world of hype, we may buy into the idea that, through Jesus, we'll be healthier and wealthier as well as wiser. So what happens when we become ill, or depressed, or bankrupt? Did we do something wrong? Has God abandoned us?

As a child, Michael Horton would run up the down escalator, trying to beat it to the top. As Christians, he notes, we sometimes seek God the same way, believing we can climb to him under our own steam. We can't, which is why we are blessed that Jesus descends to us, especially during times of trial.

In *A Place for Weakness*, formerly titled *Too Good to Be True*, Horton exposes the pop culture that sells Jesus like a product for health and happiness and reminds us that our lives often lead us on difficult routes we must follow by faith. This book offers a series of powerful readings that demonstrate how, through every type of earthly difficulty, our Father keeps his promises from Scripture and works all things together for our good.

Available in stores and online!

Pilgrim Theology

Core Doctrines for Christian Disciples

Michael Horton

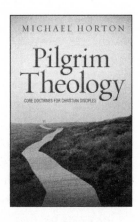

The 2011 award-winning publication *The Christian Faith* garnered wide praise as a thorough, well-informed treatment of the philosophical foundations of Christian theology, the classical elements of systematic theology, and exegesis of relevant biblical texts. *Pilgrim Theology* distills the distinctive benefits of this approach into a more accessible introduction designed for classroom and group study.

In this book, Michael Horton guides readers through a preliminary exploration of Christian theology in "a Reformed key." Horton reviews the biblical passages that give rise to a particular doctrine in addition to surveying past and present interpretations. Also included are sidebars showing the key distinctions readers need to grasp on a particular subject, helpful charts and tables illuminating exegetical and historical topics, and questions at the end of each chapter for individual, classroom, and small group reflection.

Pilgrim Theology will help undergraduate students of theology and educated laypersons gain an understanding of the Christian tradition's biblical and historical foundations.

Available in stores and online!

For Calvinism

Michael Horton

The system of theology known as Calvinism has been immensely influential for the past five hundred years, but it is often encountered negatively as a fatalistic belief system that confines human freedom and renders human action and choice irrelevant.

Taking us beyond the caricatures, Michael Horton invites us to explore the teachings of Calvinism, also commonly known as Reformed theology, by showing us how it is biblical and God-centered, leading us to live our lives for the glory of God.

Horton explores the historical roots of Calvinism, walking readers through the distinctive known as the "Five Points," and encouraging us to consider its rich resources for faith and practice in the twenty-first century.

As a companion to Roger Olson's *Against Calvinism*, readers will be able to compare contrasting perspectives and form their own opinions on the merits and weaknesses of Calvinism.

Available in stores and online!